GREAT ART IN 30 SECONDS

First published in the UK in 2017 by

Ivy Kids

An imprint of The Quarto Group
The Old Brewery
6 Blundell Street
London N7 9BH
United Kingdom
www.QuartoKnows.com

Copyright © 2017 Quarto Publishing plc

All rights reserved. No part of this book may be reproduced or transmitted in any form or by any means, electronic or mechanical, including photocopying, recording, or by any information storage-and-retrieval system, without written permission from the copyright holder.

British Library Cataloguing-in-Publication Data
A catalogue record for this book is available from the British Library.

ISBN: 978-1-78240-501-6

This book was conceived, designed & produced by

Ivy Kids

58 West Street, Brighton, BN1 2RA, United Kingdom

PUBLISHER	Susan Kelly
CREATIVE DIRECTOR	Michael Whitehead
COMMISSIONING EDITOR	Susie Behar
PROJECT EDITOR	Leah Willey
ART DIRECTOR	Hanri van Wyk
IN-HOUSE DESIGNER	Kate Haynes
DESIGNER	Emily Portnoi
EDITORIAL ASSISTANT	Lucy Menzies
PICTURE RESEARCHER	Katie Greenwood

Back cover picture credits: (top): Walters Art Museum; (bottom): Alamy/Granger Historical Picture Archive.

Printed in China

10 9 8 7 6 5 4 3 2 1

GREAT ART
IN 30 SECONDS

SUSIE HODGE

ILLUSTRATED BY WESLEY ROBINS
CONSULTANT: SIMON ARMSTRONG

IVY KIDS

Contents

About this book 6

WHAT MAKES GREAT ART? 8
Glossary 10
What is art? 12
Why does art matter? 14
What makes art valuable? 16

EARLY ART 18
Glossary 20
Prehistoric art 22
Ancient Egyptian art 24
Ancient Greek art 26
Ancient Roman art 28
Byzantine art 30
Aztec art 32

RENAISSANCE TO ROCOCO 34
Glossary 36
Early and High Renaissance art 38
Northern Renaissance art 40
Mannerist art 42
Baroque art 44
Rococo art 46

NEOCLASSICISM TO POST-IMPRESSIONISM 48
Glossary 50
Neoclassicism and Romanticism 52
Landscape and Realism 54
Ukiyo-e 56
Impressionism 58
Post-Impressionism 60

MODERN ART 62

Glossary 64

Expressionism 66

Cubism 68

Futurism 70

Dada 72

Surrealism 74

Abstract Expressionism 76

Pop art 78

Minimalism 80

CONTEMPORARY ART 82

Glossary 84

Land art 86

Conceptualism 88

New media art 90

Discover more 92

Index 94

About this book
...in 60 seconds

For thousands of years, people from all different cultures across the world have made art. Artists have carved, painted, drawn and printed. They have produced tiny works and giant constructions, from detailed pen and ink drawings, to rock carvings, paintings in frames, and huge abstract sculptures. Even before they invented writing, people created art to express their beliefs and feelings and to portray important or shocking events.

It's amazing really, but even though so many artists have made so much art, it's almost never the same. Art can be realistic or not at all. Some works seem calm and still, while others appear lively – some can even move! Art can be lovely to look at or it can be ugly. You can see artwork almost anywhere. It's found in galleries, museums and places of worship, as well as public spaces, such as hospitals, schools and parks. Art is also shown on TV and in films.

To help people understand how and why artists have worked in certain ways, art historians organize different types and styles of art into categories that we usually call art movements. You might know the term 'Renaissance', which describes art that was made in Europe in the 15th and 16th centuries. Or perhaps you have heard of Pop art, which was produced mainly in the UK and the USA during the 1960s (when pop music developed and young people between the ages of 13 and 19 were first called teenagers).

Although not all art fits into these neat categories, and art did not develop conveniently one style after the other, it can still be helpful to be able to 'place' art. The categories help you to work out roughly where, when and why a piece of art was made, just by looking at it. Art movements develop and change because of all sorts of things, including new discoveries and inventions, wars and other momentous events. Some art movements develop as a reaction against art itself. For instance, Pop art and Minimalism were reactions against Abstract Expressionism.

You do not need to know all about art to enjoy looking at it, but you might enjoy it more if you know a little about it. This book will help. It explores the fascinating story of art, beginning with the first art we know about and ending with art that was made quite recently. It looks at what has been made, who made it and what it means. Each chapter shows you different types of art, created at different times and by various artists.

Every topic has a page that explains the basics. If you are in a hurry, you can read the 3-second sum-up instead. And don't forget to try the arty missions for yourself – they'll help you create your own art.

You don't have to rush through trying to read every page quickly. You can take as long as you like to read and absorb all the information. Once you have read it, you will probably want to go back and start again, because books are like art – the more you look, the more you will see and learn.

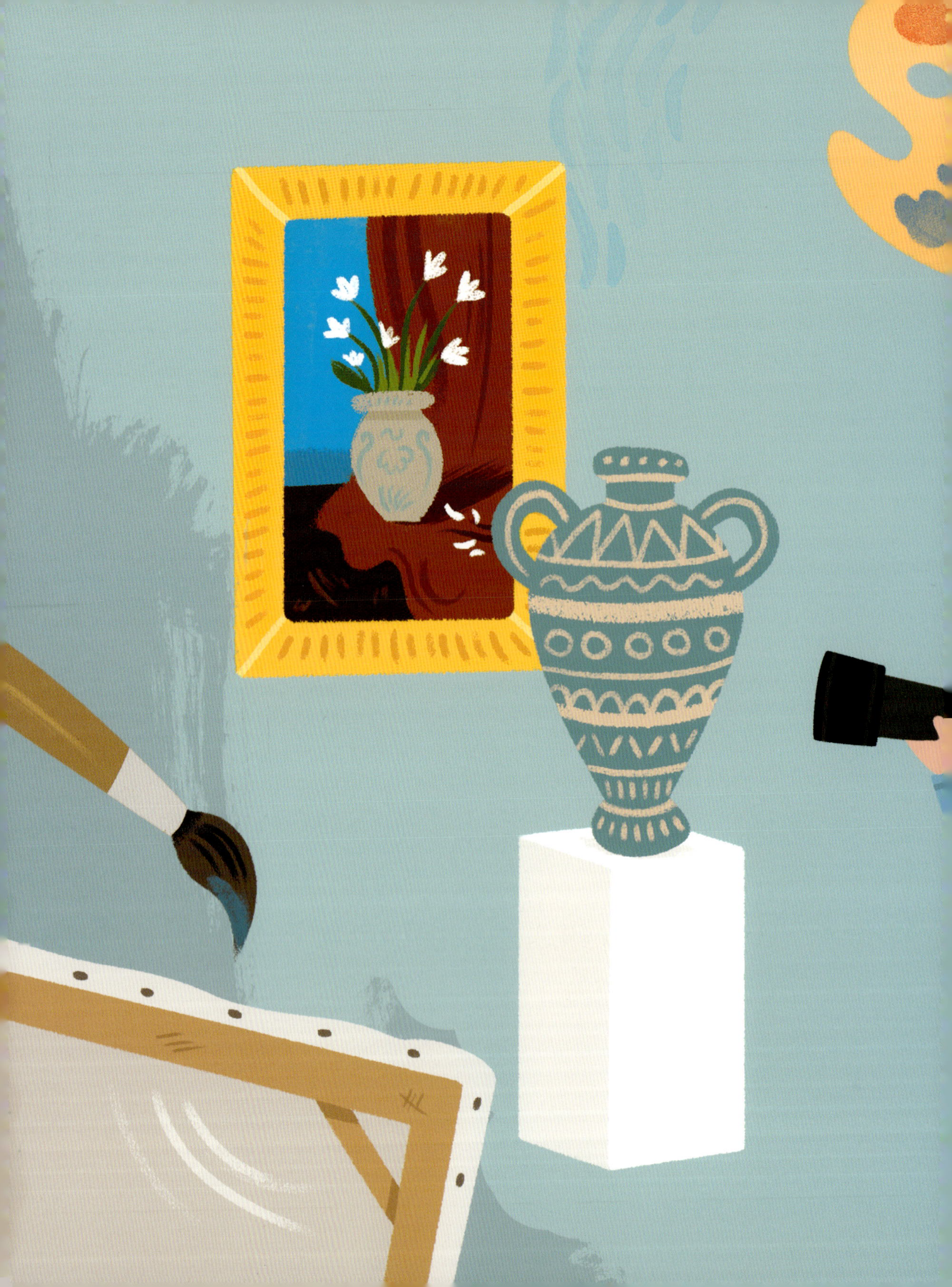

What makes great art?

As far as we know, humans have always made art – it has come in all shapes and sizes and it's been about all sorts of things, such as religion, war, love, hope and pride, or even just about colour and shape. As well as expressing strong beliefs or showing emotions or opinions, art has sometimes been a way that artists have tried to make sense of the world. For the people viewing the art, it can be both educational and emotional – it can make people feel all sorts of things, such as happy, sad, angry or shocked. Artists will probably always continue making art, and viewers will continue looking at it, buying it and talking about it.

What makes great art?
Glossary

performing arts Art forms that are performed to an audience, such as dancing, drama and music.

sculpture A three-dimensional piece of art, such as a statue, made from stone, wood, clay or another material. Sculptures can be carved (when a solid material such as stone is scraped away); cast (when a liquid material such as molten metal is poured into a mould); modelled (when a soft material is shaped); or constructed (when materials are joined together).

subject What the artist has chosen to paint, draw or sculpt.

visual arts Art forms that are created to be looked at, such as painting, **sculpture** and drawing.

11

What is art?
... in 30 seconds

People have been asking this question for hundreds of years, and there will never be just one answer! That's because art can be absolutely anything. Art is something that a person creates and it comes in many different forms, from drawings, paintings and sculptures, to carvings, pottery and buildings. Music, stories, poetry and dance performances are all types of art, too. In this book, we focus on visual art forms, such as paintings and sculptures.

There have always been many different opinions about what art should be and what it should do. Some people think that only realistic art is 'real art', while others think that there's no point making art look lifelike, because photos can do that. There are some people who believe all art should be beautiful, while others think it should show feelings and opinions, even if that makes it ugly. And then there are people who think that the message is the most important thing of all and that what the art teaches us or tells us is more important than what it looks like.

The funny thing about art is that as soon as someone tries to define what it should be, someone else will produce something that might be quite different, which proves that art can be anything. So the definition of art is always changing and there is no particular type or style of art that's best or right.

3-second sum-up
Art isn't only paintings and drawings, it's anything that a person creates to express themselves.

Art can be rubbish!
Some art really looks like rubbish. In 2007, British artist Gavin Turk made some painted bronze sculptures that looked just like bin bags. He called them *Trash*. He made them out of traditional art materials and this really made people think about what art is. They also had another strong message – they showed viewers how wasteful people can be and how we should care more for the environment.

People have always had different opinions about what art is, but really it can be anything at all.

There are all sorts of different art forms. These include visual arts such as drawing, painting and sculpture, performing arts such as dancing and acting, and a whole range of other things, including photography and writing stories or poems. Even making crafts, clothes and jewellery can be considered art.

To some people, even a rubbish bin can be art!

Why does art matter?
... in 30 seconds

Art has all sorts of important uses. You can think of it as an international language that helps people to communicate with one another. It expresses thoughts, ideas and beliefs, tells stories, spreads information and provokes emotion. It can be used in many different ways, including, for example, as propaganda (to help a cause, such as a political movement), or for religious purposes, or as decoration.

You can learn a lot from art. It always reflects the person who created it and the society it came from. You can learn about artists, their opinions, and the times and cultures that surrounded them. It can also make you think – it can pose puzzles for you to work out and even make you change your mind or attitude.

Looking at art can also make you feel something. Colours, shapes and interesting pictures and patterns can make you feel all kinds of things, such as happy and uplifted, sad or thoughtful, or even angry, shocked or a bit uncomfortable.

Art gives both our eyes and minds a workout, and when you look at art, new thoughts, feelings and dreams are often inspired.

3-second sum-up
Art can help us to make sense of the world around us.

3-minute mission Art is important!

You need: • Paper • Colouring pencils, pens or paints and paintbrushes

What is important to you? Your pet, your friends, your favourite food or place to sit, a memory? Draw it! You can draw it however you like – using colouring pencils, pens or paints. Think of your feelings as you draw and fill the paper using lots of colour and big, bold lines.

Art can teach us about different people, places, cultures and opinions.

We can learn about artists, their beliefs and their surroundings from the subjects of their art and from the materials and methods that they used to make it.

Art can bring out different emotions in people. The same artwork can make one person feel happy and another feel sad.

What makes art valuable?
... in 30 seconds

Some famous art is *really* expensive – there are paintings that have sold for hundreds of millions of pounds! But the value of art is something that people often disagree about and it changes all the time. Art that is worth very little when the artist first makes it might sell for millions years later, and some art is worth a fortune when the artist first makes it, but not much at all later on.

Some art is so expensive that it can't even be given a price. Then it's called 'priceless'. There are lots of reasons why some art is especially valuable. It's all about how much people want something and how rare it is. Artists and art styles can go in and out of fashion. Rarity also makes things valuable when a lot of people want something but only a few can actually have it. Often, it's because the artist has died, and he or she is no longer around to create more art, so the art that they created becomes rare.

Some people own very expensive art and have it in their homes, but a lot of valuable art is kept in museums and galleries. This means that experts can keep the art safe and everyone can visit the museum or gallery to look at it and enjoy it.

3-second sum-up

Art becomes valuable when it's popular or rare.

Mysterious Mona

Mystery can make art valuable too. The most famous portrait in the world, the *Mona Lisa*, was painted by Leonardo da Vinci in the early 16th century. No one knows who the woman was, what her life was like or why Leonardo painted her. People seem to like the mystery – every year, about nine million people go to see the painting in the Louvre Museum in Paris.

The value of art depends on what's in fashion and how rare it is, and it can change at any time.

Vincent van Gogh wasn't famous during his lifetime and he found it hard to make a living from his paintings.

Now, Vincent van Gogh's paintings are among the most famous and valuable in the world.

Van Gogh's most famous paintings are now so expensive that they're called 'priceless'. They're not for sale and they're displayed in galleries and museums so that everyone can see them.

Sunflowers, by Vincent van Gogh, 1888

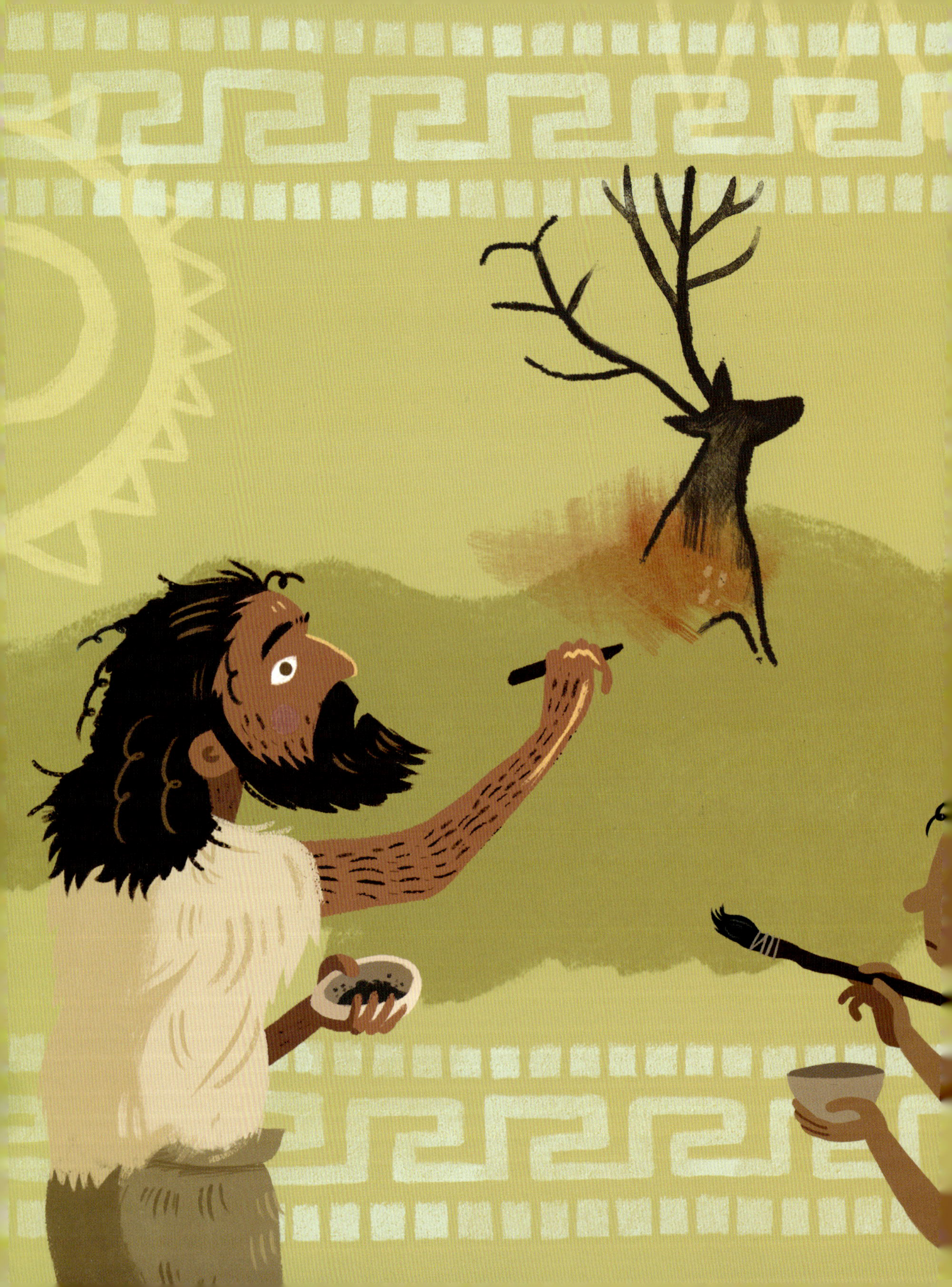

Early art

Long before humans could write, they were creating art! Early art was made in many different places around the world and it came in lots of different forms, from paintings on cave walls and inside tombs, to sculptures, pots and mosaics. People made art for all sorts of reasons and they used whatever materials they could find. A lot of ancient art was about people's religious beliefs. Making the art look realistic wasn't always the artists' aim, and sometimes the art wasn't even meant to be seen by other people.

Early art
Glossary

abstract Not realistic or lifelike.

apprentice Someone who works with a more skilled person to learn from them.

bust A **sculpture** of a person's head and shoulders.

firing The baking of pottery in a kiln (oven) to make it hard and strong.

flat painting style A style that uses blocks of colour with little shading or shadow, which makes the image look 'flat' and two-dimensional.

fresco A painting that is painted on the **plaster** of a wall or ceiling. Buon fresco is painted on wet plaster and fresco secco is painted on dry plaster.

illuminated manuscript A hand-written book, mainly made during the Middle Ages, which was decorated with gold, silver or brightly coloured borders, initials or small pictures.

mosaic A picture or pattern usually made from small pieces of stone or glass.

papyrus A type of paper – made from the papyrus plant – made by the ancient Egyptians.

pastel A soft stick of colour that can be easily smudged or blended and is used for drawing.

plaster A wet mixture that forms a smooth surface when dried. It is often spread on walls.

prehistory The period of time before writing was invented. This varies around the world, as different cultures developed writing at different times.

proportion The relationship in size of one part of something to another.

relief A picture carved in materials such as stone and wood. This makes it look like it is raised from the background.

sculpture A three-dimensional piece of art, such as a statue, made from stone, wood, clay or another material.

symbol Something that represents another thing, for example, a skull in a painting might be a symbol for death.

symmetrical When both sides of an object or image look exactly alike.

Prehistoric art
... in 30 seconds

Prehistory means before writing, so prehistoric art was made by people before the development of writing. Humans have lived on Earth for over four million years, but the earliest art that's been found was made about 35,000 years ago: small stone statues of women with round bellies and no feet or hands were unearthed in a cave in Germany by a team of archaeologists. Art may have been made even before this time, but it has either rotted away or been destroyed – or we just haven't found it yet!

Prehistoric art has been discovered all over the world – in Europe, Africa, North and South America, Asia and Australia. Although it's spread out across so many different places, a lot of it is surprisingly similar. Prehistoric artists often created pictures or carvings of animals, painting or scratching them onto cave walls or making them out of rock or bone.

We know little about these artists because they couldn't write anything down, so no one is completely sure who they were, why they made their art or what it was supposed to mean. But the art does still tell us a bit about the way they looked at the world and about what was important to them, including things like families and hunting animals for food.

3-second sum-up
Art has been made since prehistoric times, which is the time before people had even invented writing.

3-minute mission Be a cave artist

You need: • Black, grey or brown paper • Pastels or paints and paintbrushes

Using a large sheet of black, grey or brown paper and some pastels or paints, create a picture of your favourite animal or your pet. Draw the animal from the side like the cave artists did. Use 'earth' colours, such as browns, yellows, greys, black and white. Try to rub, smudge and blend your colours, too.

People have made art for thousands of years, and prehistoric paintings and sculptures tell us a little about the life of early artists.

Artists made paintings and carvings about things that were important to them, like animals and family.

Some made handprints by holding their hands flat against cave walls and blowing coloured powder over them through hollow bones.

Artists used plants and minerals, such as charcoal, earth and chalk, and mixed them with animal fat, water or even spit or blood to make paint.

With no brushes, they used sticks, bones, fur, leaves or their fingers to apply paint.

Top: Prehistoric cave painting at the Lascaux cave, France, made 20,000–17,000 years ago
Bottom: Prehistoric cave painting at the Cave of the Hands in Patagonia, Argentina, made 13,000–9,000 years ago

Ancient Egyptian art
... in 30 seconds

The Egyptians lived about 5,000 years ago, and their civilization was one of the most advanced in the ancient world. As well as worshipping hundreds of gods and goddesses, they believed in an afterlife. We know this from the colourful tomb paintings and other art they left behind.

Egyptian art followed strict rules. It took many years to learn and some apprentice artists began their training at the age of nine. Although the flat painting style the artists used looks strange to us now, it made perfect sense to them. Following the formula was more important to an Egyptian artist than making a picture look lifelike or unique. Every painting was measured out precisely and included only the most essential items.

Whether it was wall art, a statue or a painting on papyrus, Egyptian art was usually made to honour a wealthy or important person, such as a pharaoh, who had died. The Egyptians believed their gods helped the dead travel to the afterlife, where they could live in spirit form. So, to show the gods how someone had spent their life, their body was put inside a tomb and surrounded by art. Richly carved stone figures and hieroglyphs – little pictures or symbols that stand for an object or word – as well as beautiful wall paintings displayed scenes from the person's life.

3-second sum-up

Ancient Egyptians made art to show the gods how important people had spent their lives.

3-minute mission Tell an Egyptian story

You need: • Paper • Colouring pencils or pens

Make your own ancient Egyptian picture. What do you do from the time you wake up to the time you start school? Draw it in a series of small pictures, but in Egyptian style, with heads, arms and legs drawn from the side, and chests and eyes drawn from the front. Colour it all in with smooth, bright blocks of colour and no shading.

Animals and flowers were quite realistic.

Ancient Egyptian art was created to help wealthy dead people reach the afterlife, and it followed a set of strict rules.

Heads were drawn from the side, eyes from the front.

Arms and legs were drawn from the side, chests from the front.

Plaster was smoothed over the walls, before a trainee artist marked out a grid of squares using string soaked in paint.

Other trainee artists drew the scene in the grid, copying from a picture.

A senior artist then made corrections and added details, before another senior artist painted the picture in bright colours.

Fowling in the marshes, a wall painting from an Egyptian tomb, c. 1350 BCE

Ancient Greek art
... in 30 seconds

Art was important to the ancient Greeks, who lived around 2,500 years ago. Greek artists decorated homes with paintings, made beautiful pottery, designed impressive buildings and created grand sculptures. Ancient Greeks wanted to make art that looked as perfect to them as things are in nature. They achieved this by using proportion.

Early Greek statues often looked stiff and unreal, but at about the end of the 6th century BCE, artists began to study and measure the proportions of the human body. This changed everything. Using exact measurements, sculptors could create natural-looking statues that equalled their idea of perfection. Artists and architects ever since have been influenced by this way of thinking.

Although few Greek paintings still exist, a lot of pottery has survived. There are two main styles: black-figure and red-figure. Black-figure pottery was made by painting pictures and patterns onto red clay pots using slip (watery clay). After firing, the slip turned black but the background stayed red. In red-figure pottery, the background was painted with slip, leaving the patterns and pictures red.

3-second sum-up

Ancient Greek artists tried to make their art look perfect and flawless.

3-minute mission Make a Greek tile

You need: • Self-drying clay • Rolling pin • Plastic ruler • Pencil • Paints and paintbrushes • PVA glue

The ancient Greeks used clay to make pots, vases and tiles. Make your own Greek tile using self-drying clay. Roll out a piece of clay and cut it into a square with the edge of a plastic ruler. 'Draw' on it using a pencil point. When the clay has hardened, paint it, and then coat it with PVA glue that dries clear and shiny.

Ancient Greek artists aimed to create pottery, sculptures and architecture that were precise and well-proportioned.

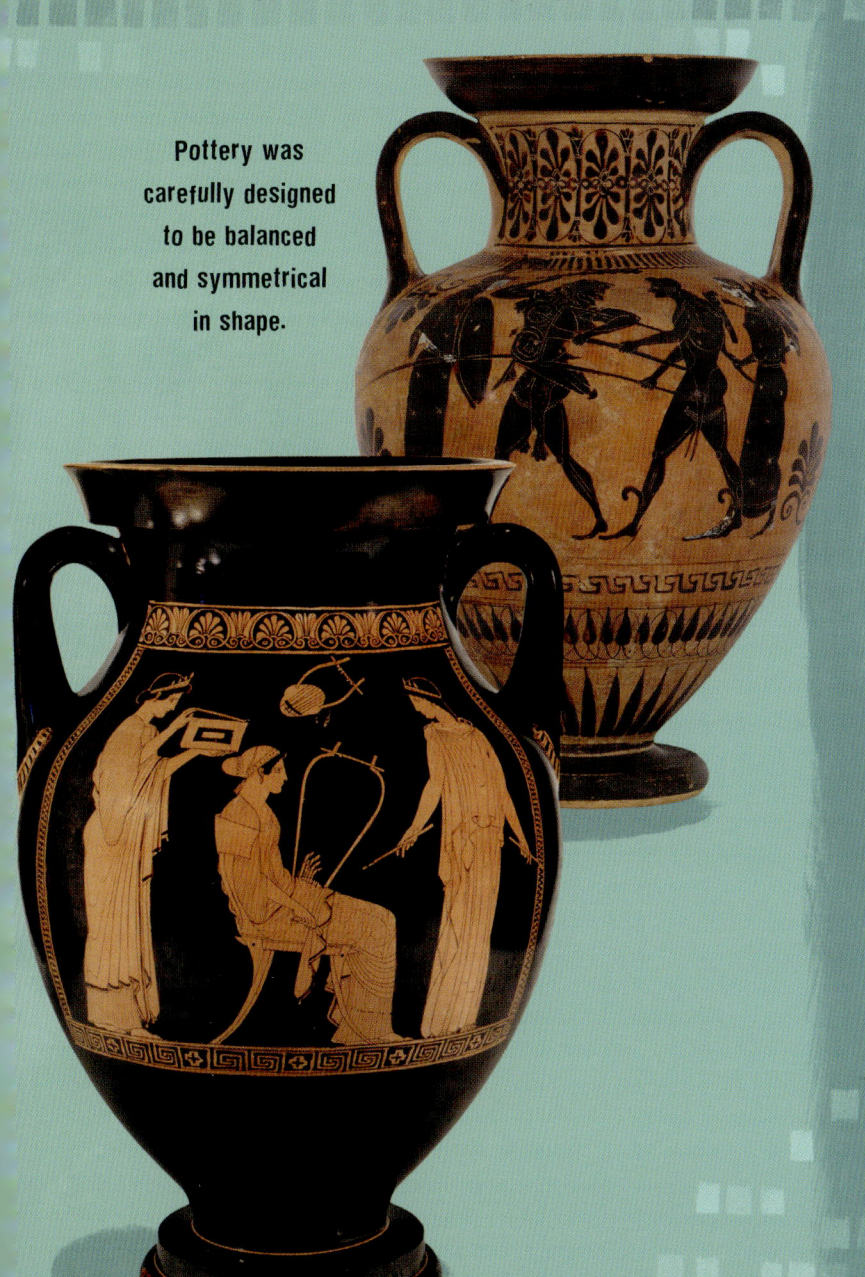

Pottery was carefully designed to be balanced and symmetrical in shape.

Statues were often carved in white marble. Artists wanted them to look as lifelike, and as perfect, as possible.

Ancient Greek temples followed strict rules for design and strength and they were also precisely measured.

Top: Black-figure pot showing Herakles and Apollo fighting, c. 520 BCE
Bottom: Red-figure pot showing Sappho (a Greek poet) teaching a music lesson, c. 460–450 BCE

Ancient Roman art
... in 30 seconds

By 100 CE, the powerful Roman Empire had conquered huge parts of the world. The Roman rulers built cities in their new lands, and employed architects, craftspeople and artists to fill the cities with buildings and art.

Ancient Roman artists learned from ancient Greek art and many Roman sculptures were copies of Greek statues. Unlike Greek artists, who aimed for an ideal of beauty and perfection, Roman artists often made art that was closer to real life. For example, when they sculpted someone, they included their imperfections, such as wrinkles or a misshapen nose.

Most Roman art was used to show power, and sculptures were everywhere – in streets, temples, parks and rich people's homes. Having huge statues of the emperor placed around the city was a good way to remind everyone who was in charge. Artists also made statues of the Roman gods and goddesses, respected philosophers (thinkers), famous athletes and army generals. In addition, the Romans made pottery, reliefs (raised, carved pictures), frescoes (wall paintings) and mosaics.

3-second sum-up

Ancient Roman art was lifelike and was often made to display the power of the Empire.

3-minute mission Make a mosaic

You need: • Plain paper or card • Coloured paper • Scissors • Pencil • Glue

The Romans used stone and glass to make mosaics, but you can use coloured paper. Cut your coloured paper into small squares and draw a picture or pattern on a large sheet of plain paper or card. Then glue your small squares onto your design, leaving tiny spaces in between.

As the Roman Empire spread around the world, Roman art was used to show power and status.

Some fresco paintings were designed to look like windows with views out to beautiful scenery.

Roman reliefs often showed big battles and other important events.

Romans made mosaics mainly for their floors. The earliest were only black and white, but later they were colourful.

Lifelike busts of emperors and senators were dotted around Roman cities, reminding people who was in charge.

Bust of the emperor Hadrian, c. 117–138 CE

Byzantine art
... in 30 seconds

From around 500 to 1000 CE, Christianity spread through Europe. The first Roman emperor to follow the new religion was called Constantine. He moved the capital of the Roman Empire from Rome to Byzantium (now Istanbul, Turkey) in around 300 CE, and named it Constantinople (after himself). The art that developed there became known as Byzantine art.

Byzantine art was religious art that often showed images from the Bible, known as icons. Most people at the time couldn't read, so the pictures reminded them what they should think of while they were praying. The art was highly decorative, with artists creating impressive frescoes and delicate mosaics on church walls, detailed stained-glass windows, religious manuscripts embellished with gold, and paintings made on wooden panels with bright colours.

Byzantine art was not meant to look realistic. This was to prevent Christians from worshipping pictures or statues of biblical figures. If art looked too realistic, there was a risk that people would worship the art rather than the holy figures themselves.

3-second sum-up
Byzantine art was unrealistic and decorative, and it depicted Christian figures.

3-minute mission Illuminated letters

You need: • Plain paper or card • Pencil • Ruler • Colouring pencils or pens

Illuminated manuscripts were a popular form of Byzantine art. The first letters on a page were usually larger than the rest, brightly coloured and with pictures or patterns around them. Make your own illuminated initials! On a piece of paper or card, carefully draw your initials – you can use a ruler if you like. Then decorate them with pictures and patterns, and colour them in.

Byzantine art focused on Christianity and the Bible, aiming to help people pray and worship.

Artists purposely made their art look flat and unrealistic by painting people facing the front, without shadows.

Artists never showed smiling faces!

Illuminated manuscripts were created by priests and monks. They were detailed and colourful, with lots of pictures and patterns.

Mosaic of the *Virgin Mary and Child* at Chora Church, Istanbul, Turkey, c. 1315–21 CE

Aztec art

... in 30 seconds

Over 200 years, from the 14th to the 16th centuries, several Aztec civilizations developed in Central Mexico. These included the Olmec, Maya, Inca, Toltec and Zapotec. Each civilization created its own type of art.

Although the Aztecs developed their own style of art, they were also influenced by the art of tribes who had lived in the area for thousands of years. This meant that Aztec art varied greatly. It featured gods, people, animals and plants, and it was sometimes natural-looking and sometimes colourful and abstract. It included stone sculptures, carvings, pottery, metalwork and jewellery, masks and architecture.

Aztec art was made mainly to honour the civilizations' many gods. The Aztecs placed huge stone statues of gods inside temples and created detailed carvings and reliefs on stone walls and pillars. Even pottery that was used to hold food and drink was made in designs that honoured the gods.

The Aztecs were farming people, and their gods represented the natural world around them, including animals and the weather. Their most important god was the god of the Sun, and there were lots of different versions of this god. The earliest of these was called Nanahuatzin. He was replaced by Huitzilopochtli, who was also the god of war.

3-second sum-up

Aztec art developed over thousands of years and was made mainly to celebrate the Aztec gods.

Aztec pictographs

The Aztecs developed their own form of writing. Aztec priests – not ordinary Aztecs – developed this writing, following the language they spoke. Instead of writing shapes for letters, Aztec writing used symbols or pictures, called glyphs or pictographs, to represent things, such as objects or sounds. Priests wrote these pictographs on long sheets called codexes. These were made of animal skins or plant fibres.

Sculptures, buildings and pottery were all made to honour the Aztec gods.

TEPEYOLLOTL,
the jaguar god –
god of the night sky.

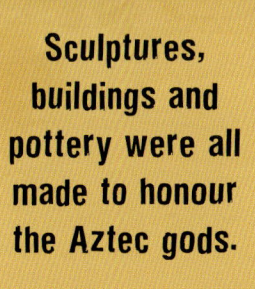

QUETZALCOATL,
the snake god –
god of the wind.

HUITZILOPOCHTLI,
the hummingbird god –
god of the Sun and god of war.

XOLOTL,
linked to dogs –
god of fire.

Sculpture of an Aztec maize god, c. 1400–1521 CE

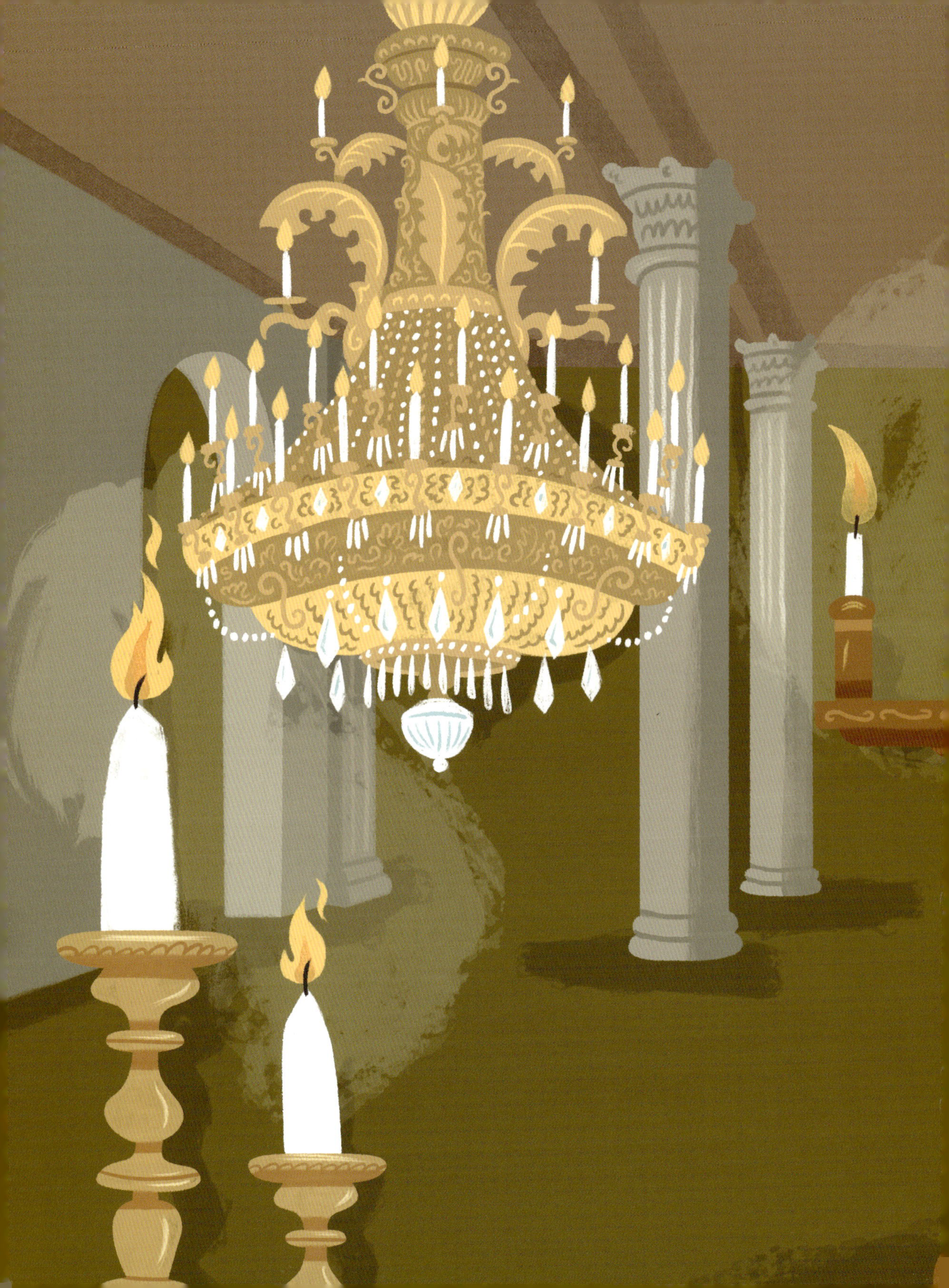

Renaissance to Rococo

During the 15th century in Europe, some of the art and writings of ancient Greece and Rome were rediscovered. In Italy in particular, for the first time in centuries, many ancient principles in technology, science, maths, writing and art were revived, and this soon spread across Europe. This period was later called the Renaissance, which means 'rebirth' in French. In the 16th century, some artists tried a new style that became known as Mannerism, and by the 17th century, another dramatic art style developed: the Baroque. Most Renaissance, Mannerist and Baroque art was quite serious and focused mainly on Christianity. In the early 18th century, Rococo art emerged and this was more playful and all about having fun.

Renaissance to Rococo
Glossary

classical Relating to the Ancient Greeks' and Romans' art and way of life.

convex Curving outwards, like the outside of a bowl.

engraving A drawing scratched into a surface, such as a metal plate. The plate is covered in ink and used to make **prints**.

flat colour Blocks of colour with little shading or shadow, which look 'flat' and **two-dimensional**.

interior design The decoration of the spaces inside a building.

landscape A painting of natural scenery, such as mountains, trees, the sea and the sky.

myth A traditional story that is not true, and often involves a hero and gods and goddesses.

oil paint Paint made from mixing **pigments** and oil.

perspective A way of drawing that shows depth and distance; this gives the impression that something drawn on a **two-dimensional** surface is **three-dimensional**.

pigment The part of the paint that gives it colour. Early painters used pigments from ground-up minerals, plants and insects, but today pigments are mainly made from chemicals.

portrait A picture or a **sculpture** of a person.

print An image made by pressing a carved block or plate, covered in ink or paint, on to paper. This technique allows lots of copies to be made of the same image. **Woodcuts** and **engravings** are types of prints.

proportion The relationship in size of one part of something to another.

sculpture A **three-dimensional** piece of art, such as a statue, made from stone, wood, clay or another material.

tempera paint Paint made from mixing **pigments**, egg and water.

three-dimensional (3D) Something that is not flat; it has height, depth and width.

two-dimensional (2D) Something that is flat; it has height and width, but not depth.

woodcut A drawing carved into a block of wood. The block is covered in ink or paint and used to make **prints**.

Early and High Renaissance art ... in 30 seconds

During the 15th century, some artists and thinkers in Italy rediscovered ancient Greek and Roman art and writing. It inspired them to create their own artistic style, which was later called Renaissance art. Renaissance art is usually split into Early Renaissance art and High Renaissance art.

Unlike Byzantine art, Early Renaissance art (roughly the 15th century) aimed to be realistic and show emotion. The discovery of perspective also helped two-dimensional (2D) paintings to look three-dimensional (3D) by making distant objects smaller. Famous Italian Early Renaissance artists include Donatello, who created lifelike sculptures, and Botticelli, who often painted classical myths.

Leonardo da Vinci 1452–1519

During the High Renaissance (approximately from 1490 to the 1520s), artists – still mainly Italian – invented even more skilful methods to show the 3D world in 2D paintings and to show emotion, realism and drama in both paintings and sculptures. They used light and shadow to skilfully create contrast and depth. There were several artist geniuses working during the High Renaissance, including Leonardo da Vinci, Michelangelo, Raphael and Titian, who all used new techniques. Leonardo da Vinci, for instance, used sfumato, a technique of shading colours softly to make things look especially 3D.

3-second sum-up

Inspired by ancient Greek and Roman art, Renaissance artists used new techniques to make lifelike art.

3-minute mission Make a picture in perspective

You need: • Paper • Pencil

Draw a horizontal line across a piece of paper. This is your horizon, or where the sky meets the land or sea. Mark a point in the middle of this line – this is the vanishing point. The closer everything in your drawing gets to that point, the smaller it should be. Draw a scene, following this rule.

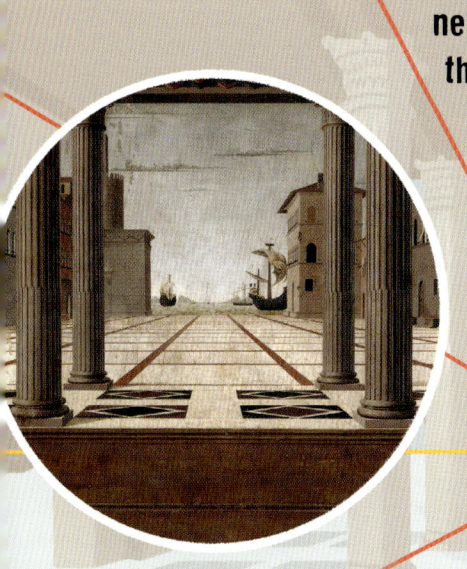

Renaissance artists used new techniques to make their art more realistic than ever.

2D pictures were drawn and painted using rules of perspective that helped to make them look 3D.

This is the horizon line (where the land appears to meet the sky).

This is the vanishing point (a point on the horizon line where all of the objects in the picture vanish).

The closer to the vanishing point objects get, the smaller they appear. This makes them look further away.

It took Michelangelo four years to paint the ceiling of the Sistine Chapel – one of the most famous High Renaissance works of art.

The ceiling is filled with over 300 life-sized figures. They are all in dramatic poses, with strong, muscular bodies.

Top: *Architectural Veduta*, by Francesco di Giorgio Martini, c. 1490
Bottom: *The Creation of Adam*, by Michelangelo, Sistine Chapel, c. 1512

Northern Renaissance art
... in 30 seconds

From 1430 to 1580, a new style of art emerged in northern Europe. Instead of being inspired by ancient Greek and Roman art like the Italian Renaissance artists, Northern Renaissance artists were inspired by the world around them.

Artists in the Netherlands, such as Pieter Bruegel the Elder, studied nature and created lifelike paintings of the living world. No one knows exactly when oil paints were first used, but some time during the 15th century, artists in the Netherlands mixed their dry powdered pigments with oil rather than egg. Unlike the tempera paints that artists had been using before, oil paints are slow to dry, which gave artists time to alter or improve things as they worked, adding details and creating more realistic pictures. Tempera is opaque, but oil paint dries with a semi-transparent sheen.

Artists in northern Europe such as Albrecht Dürer, Pieter Bruegel the Elder, Jan van Eyck, Robert Campin and Hans Holbein the Younger created a range of art with incredibly lifelike details. Many artists painted on smooth wooden panels, which helped them create realistic details. Some made woodcut prints and some made wood carvings.

3-second sum-up

Northern Renaissance artists produced extremely detailed, lifelike art using oil paint, as well as making prints and carvings.

Printing and printmaking

In c. 1440 in Germany, Johannes Gutenberg invented the printing press. This meant that books could be made and sold cheaply, so more people were able to read and learn about things. Also in northern Europe, art printmaking developed, particularly woodcuts and engravings. To make woodcuts, artists carved away parts of a shallow block of wood with sharp tools, leaving raised areas that made the print.

Colours, shadows and highlights could be blended smoothly with oil paints.

Northern Renaissance artists closely observed the natural world so that they were able to create lifelike artwork.

Instead of huge works of art for churches, smaller paintings were made for rich traders to buy and display at home.

Artists were especially skilful at carving and printing woodcut pictures, paying close attention to detail.

Top: *Hunters in the Snow*, by Pieter Bruegel the Elder, 1565
Bottom: *The Flight into Egypt*, by Albrecht Dürer, c. 1504

Mannerist art

... in 30 seconds

From the 1520s to about 1600 a style of art called Mannerism emerged. The word 'Mannerism' comes from the Italian word 'maniera', meaning manner or style, but it was not used to describe the style until 200 years later.

Although it was still inspired by ancient Greek and Roman art, Mannerist art was more exaggerated and unusual. As opposed to looking balanced and natural, people, animals and objects were often drawn slightly out of proportion. People were shown with graceful but strangely long arms, legs and bodies, and very small heads. They were also often in complex and twisted poses and the paintings were often in unnatural colours.

Some people believe that this unusual style was the result of the religious and political turmoil experienced during the Reformation. During this turbulent period, the Catholic Church split and a new type of Christianity, called Protestantism, emerged. Other people believe that Mannerism was inspired by the extravagant, exaggerated and showy royal courts of the 16th century.

One well-known Mannerist is El Greco. He came from Greece and his real name was Doménikos Theotokópoulos, but he lived and worked in Spain, so was nicknamed El Greco, meaning 'the Greek' in Spanish.

3-second sum-up

Mannerists exaggerated and elongated figures in their paintings and sculptures.

3-minute mission Distorted self-portrait

You need: • Paper • Spoon • Pencil

When the Italian artist Parmigianino was 21, he painted his own portrait from his reflection in a convex mirror. The painting has no straight lines and parts of him look really odd. Draw your own distorted reflection by looking into the back of a spoon. Look closely at your face and everything behind you and copy what you see.

Mannerist paintings often looked exaggerated, with people and animals appearing extra tall and elegant.

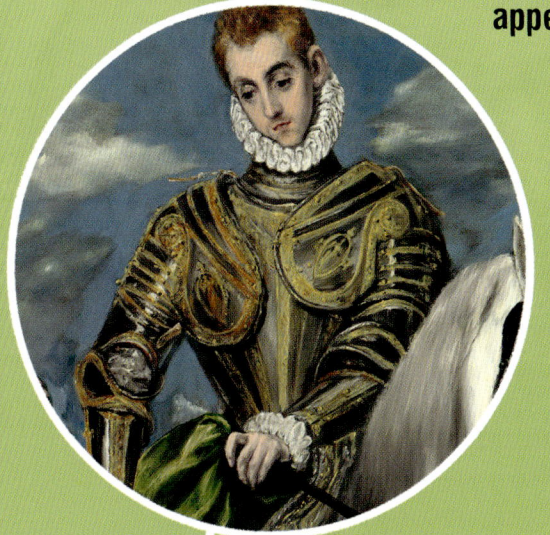

The legs of this horse have been elongated.

The man's head has been made much smaller than in real life. This contrasts with his long body.

This female saint's hands are large, contrasting with her small head.

Top and middle: *Saint Martin and the Beggar*, by El Greco, 1597–99
Bottom: *The Virgin and Child with St Martina and St Agnes*, by El Greco, 1597–99

Baroque art
... in 30 seconds

In early 17th-century Europe, the Protestant Church was becoming more popular. The Catholic Church had lost influence and wanted to attract Christians back to its church, so its leaders encouraged artists to create art that told Bible stories in dramatic ways. This theatrical style became known as Baroque art.

The Baroque movement began in Italy and later spread to other parts of the world. As well as paintings, sculpture and architecture, the Baroque included music. All Baroque art is expressive, full of life and often emotional. Paintings by Caravaggio and Rembrandt show real-looking people in exciting ways, created to thrill 17th-century viewers.

Rembrandt Harmenszoon van Rijn 1606-69

Baroque paintings often had dark backgrounds with bright light illuminating the main parts of the picture. This technique – called chiaroscuro – created a sense of drama. Sculptures were impressive and dramatic too, often made from expensive materials such as marble or bronze, and sometimes even covered with gold.

3-second sum-up

Baroque art was dramatic and theatrical, and was encouraged by the Catholic Church to make Catholicism more attractive.

3-minute mission Chiaroscuro

You need: • Objects to draw • Lamp or torch • White paper • Pencil • Colouring pencils or paints and paintbrushes

To make your own picture in chiaroscuro, gather some objects together, such as fruit or vegetables, or perhaps bottles or bowls, and arrange them on a table. Make the room dark and put a small lamp or torch to one side of your arrangement. Draw the outline of what you see, marking the areas of shadow, light and highlight. Then make the room light again, and colour your picture using colouring pencils or paints, exaggerating the dark shadows and leaving the highlights white.

Baroque art used new painting techniques to create dramatic, emotional and appealing art.

This painting by Caravaggio depicts a Bible story using lifelike people.

Some people didn't like Caravaggio's art because his lifelike biblical figures looked poor, not rich and beautiful, which was shocking for the time.

Some artists used a technique called chiaroscuro: dramatically contrasting light and dark.

Light source

Highlight

Shadow

Light

Cast shadow

The Denial of Saint Peter, by Caravaggio, 1610

Rococo art
... in 30 seconds

In around 1715, a group of French artists began painting in a light and graceful way, often using pastel colours. This playful style was partly a reaction to the drama and darkness of the Baroque art that had come before it. It became known as Rococo, probably from the French word 'rocaille' (which describes shells and rocks), because it used lots of natural patterns and shapes.

First appearing in interior design and architecture, the style was soon also seen in paintings and sculpture. Rococo paintings were cheerful and elegant, often showing aristocrats having fun, playing music, dancing and picnicking. Rococo artists often painted imaginary, dreamy landscapes, flattering portraits, and themes of love and romance. Serious things such as religion and politics no longer took centre stage as they had in Baroque art.

Famous Rococo artists include Jean-Antoine Watteau and François Boucher. Watteau often painted wealthy aristocrats in settings inspired by the natural world. Boucher was well-known for his picturesque landscape paintings, which often included shepherds and shepherdesses in luxurious clothes.

3-second sum-up
Using soft colours and curving lines, Rococo art focused on nature and rich people enjoying themselves.

3-minute mission Design a Rococo chandelier

You need: • Paper • Pencil • Colouring pencils

Try designing your own Rococo chandelier. Draw your design lightly in pencil, filling the page. Include plenty of curves, and scroll, shell or leaf designs. Add candles (as electricity hadn't been invented yet) and then colour it carefully.

Rococo artists used elegant designs and pastel colours to create light and playful art.

In this painting, Watteau shows a woman in a realistic way, but her surroundings (and the lion sitting next to her!) make the painting feel dreamlike.

The Rococo art movement began in interior design and architecture, and was inspired by natural shapes, such as shells and leaves.

Ceres (Summer), by Jean-Antoine Watteau, c. 1717–18

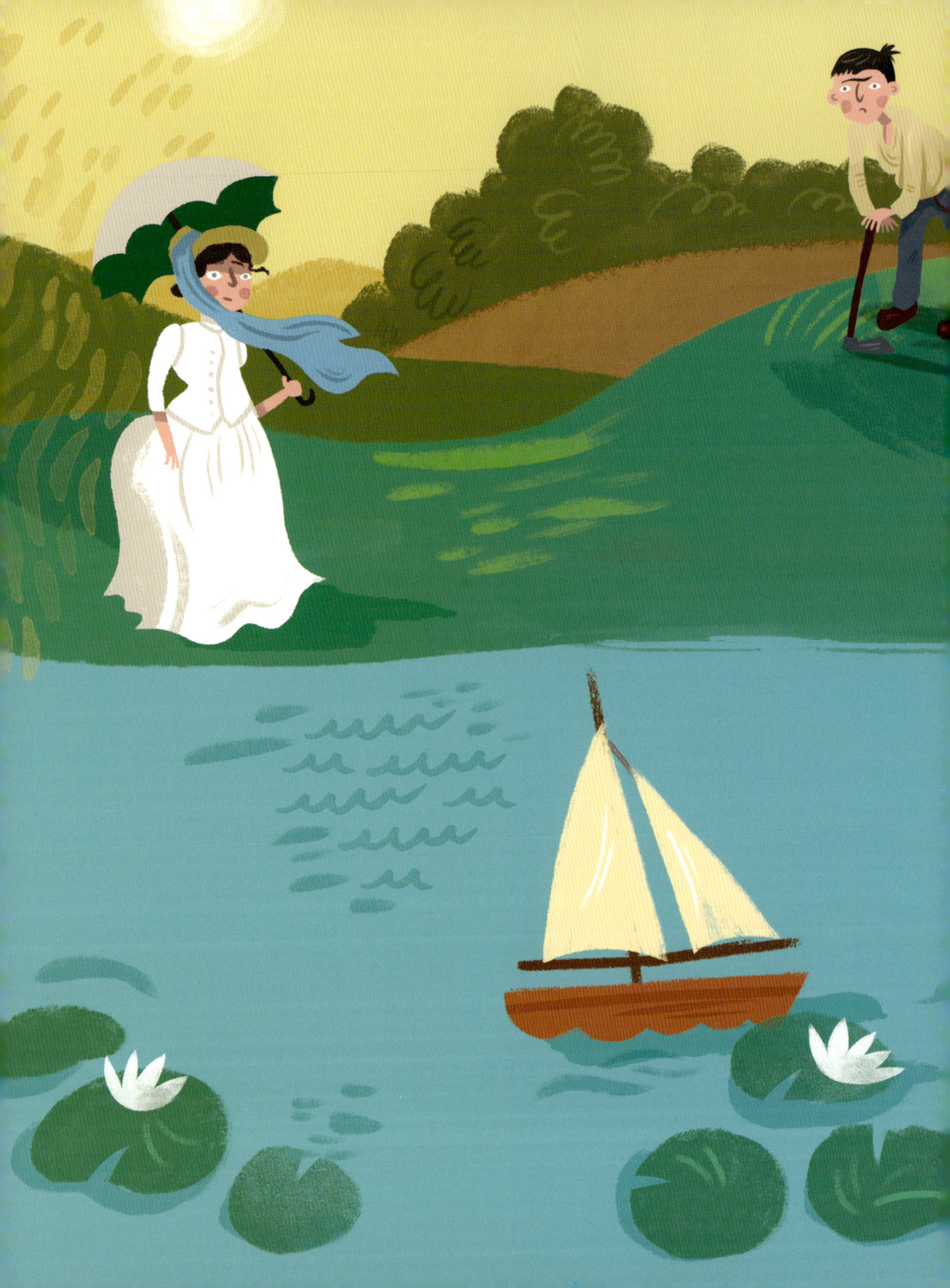

Neoclassicism to Post-Impressionism

Art changed in the 18th century with the Baroque and Rococo, but there were even more changes in the 19th century. The Industrial Revolution spread in Europe and the USA, transforming society and the economy, and leading to the growth of towns and cities. Tin paint tubes were invented in 1841, which meant that artists no longer had the messy, fiddly job of grinding and mixing their own paints. They could buy oil paints ready mixed in tin tubes, which were easy to carry and use, and made it easier for artists to paint the changing world around them. These developments encouraged artists to experiment and, as they came up with novel ideas, new art movements were born.

Neoclassicism to Post-Impressionism
Glossary

art movement A group of artists producing a similar style or type of art at a certain time.

asymmetrical An object or image that is not identical on both sides.

classical Relating to the Ancient Greeks' and Romans' art and way of life.

composition The way of arranging the different parts of a picture.

exhibition A display of works of art, generally held in a gallery or museum.

Industrial Revolution A time of huge changes in industry, agriculture and science in Britain in the late 18th and early 19th centuries, which spread to other countries.

landscape A painting of natural scenery, such as mountains, trees, the sea and the sky.

mass-produced Made in large amounts, often by machinery.

oil paint Paint made by mixing pigments (colours) and oil.

portable Able to be carried.

portrait A picture or a sculpture of a person.

print An image made by pressing a carved block or plate, covered in ink or paint, on to paper. This technique allows lots of copies to be made of the same image.

subject What the artist has chosen to paint, draw or sculpt.

symbol Something that represents another thing, for example, a skull in a painting might be a symbol for death.

watercolour Thin, semi-transparent paint made by mixing pigments (colours) with water. The term also describes paintings created using watercolour paints.

woodblock A carved block of wood used to make **prints**.

Neoclassicism and Romanticism
... in 30 seconds

The late 18th and early 19th centuries were a time of new ideas, fascinating discoveries and turbulent rebellions. The influence of all this led to two different art movements.

Neoclassical – 'New Classical'– art was inspired by the excavations of ancient Roman towns in Italy, such as Pompeii. Paintings, sculptures, buildings and everyday objects were uncovered at the ancient sites, leading to a new curiosity about ancient Roman 'classical' art.

Neoclassical artists include Jacques-Louis David and Jean-Auguste-Dominique Ingres, who drew smooth outlines and portrayed noble figures. Artists aimed to inspire courage and pride, and were proud of the control and skill their work displayed. Another French artist, Elisabeth Louise Vigée Le Brun, painted with Rococo colours and a smooth Neoclassical style.

Passionate, dramatic and lively, Romanticism was a reaction to the troubles and turbulence of the time, as well as to the new interest in Rome. Romantic artists include French painters Eugène Delacroix and Théodore Géricault and Spanish artist Francisco de Goya. They used bold colours and sweeping, visible brushstrokes to create emotional, imaginative artwork.

Elisabeth Louise Vigée Le Brun
1755–1842

3-second sum-up
Neoclassicism was calm, careful and precise, while Romanticism was dramatic, bold and imaginative.

Deadly art
During this period, some of the paints that artists used were literally killing them. Accidentally licking certain paints was deadly, while others even made the air around them dangerous. Some brown paints were made by grinding up ancient Egyptian mummies stolen from their tombs, and a certain shade of green paint was made with poisonous copper arsenite that was also used to kill rats in Paris sewers. A colour called 'Indian yellow' was made from the wee of a type of Indian cow – it was both unhealthy and smelly!

At a time of great discoveries and rebellions, two new art styles developed: Neoclassicism and Romanticism.

NEOCLASSICISM

Began: 1780s

Popular subjects: Portraits inspired by Greek and Roman history

Mood: Calm, patriotic, noble

Style: Precise drawing, smooth outlines and careful shading

Aim: To inspire courage and pride

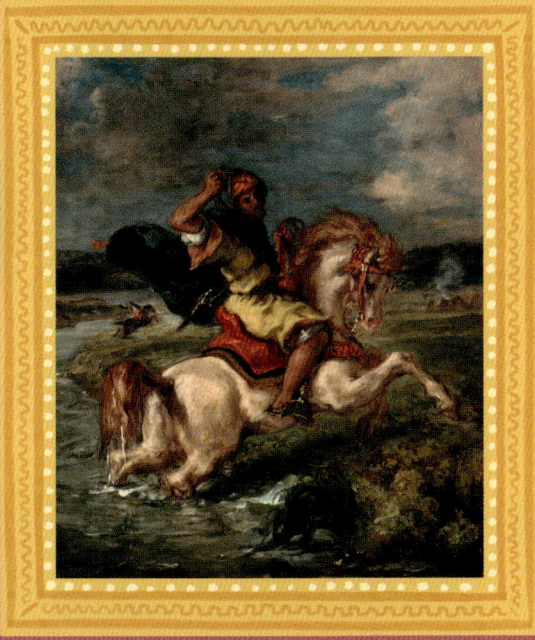

ROMANTICISM

Began: 1800s

Popular subjects: Legends, nature, violence

Mood: Dramatic, emotional, lively

Style: Sweeping, visible brushstrokes and bold colours

Aim: To inspire emotion and the imagination

Top: *Napoleon Crossing the Alps*, by Jacques-Louis David, 1800
Bottom: *Moroccan Horseman Crossing a Ford*, by Eugène Delacroix, c. 1850

Landscape and Realism
... in 30 seconds

During the early 19th century, the Industrial Revolution changed people's lives forever. Machines made goods cheaply in factories, trains sped across the land, and cities grew as huge numbers of people moved away from the countryside. This upheaval prompted many artists to view the world differently.

Most people at this time believed great art should show historic events or famous people, but some artists began to paint the landscapes they saw from the new trains. The English painters J. M. W. Turner and John Constable are sometimes known as Romantic landscape artists. Turner painted the effects of light and atmosphere, and Constable's paintings showed the countryside he especially loved.

Realism started in France. It shocked people because it often showed the hard lives of poor people instead of the comfortable lives of wealthy people. By now, paints came in portable tubes and Realist artists such as Édouard Manet, Jean-François Millet and Gustave Courbet could work away from their studios, painting the people and places they saw in the new modern world.

3-second sum-up

Some artists painted reality as they saw it around them, showing life at the time, not fancy subjects and styles.

3-minute mission Watercolour landscape

You need: • Thick paper • Sponge or brush • Paints and paintbrushes • Paper towel or cotton wool • Pencil or pen

Wet a thick sheet of paper with a damp sponge or brush. Paint a wash of blue on the paper – use very watery paint, adding more water as you work down the page. While it's still wet, press scrunched-up paper towel or cotton wool onto the top of the page and then lift it off to make clouds. Paint different shades of green from the bottom to the middle of the paper, so it overlaps with some of the blue. When both colours are dry, add trees, flowers, birds or a winding path, using a pencil or a pen.

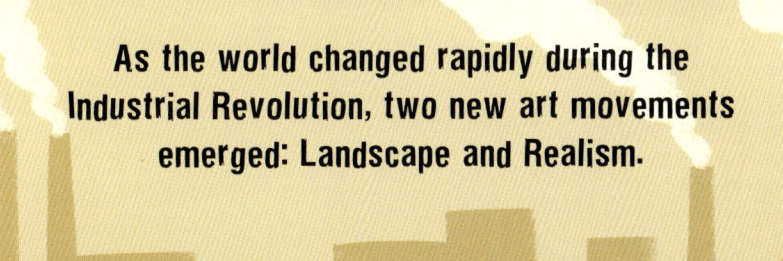

As the world changed rapidly during the Industrial Revolution, two new art movements emerged: Landscape and Realism.

Landscape artists began painting everyday landscapes, instead of focusing on famous people and important events.

The 19th-century Realists painted the ordinary modern world as it really was, with no symbols or imaginative elements.

Millet had great sympathy for the poor and often showed their hard lives in his paintings.

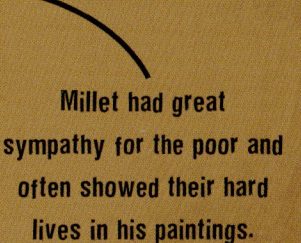

Man with a Hoe, by Jean-François Millet, 1860–62

Ukiyo-e
... in 30 seconds

Ukiyo-e describes pictures of everyday life in Japan, made from the 17th to the 19th centuries. Ukiyo means 'the world of ordinary people' and e means 'picture'. Ukiyo-e art often features flat-looking colour and an asymmetrical composition.

Ukiyo-e art became popular in Japan in the 1620s, when many people moved from the countryside into cities. The earliest ukiyo-e pictures showed popular entertainments, such as traditional actors and sumo wrestlers, in the city of Kyoto (the old capital of Japan). Later ukiyo-e subjects included landscapes, heroes and folk tales.

In the 18th century, ukiyo-e artists such as Kitagawa Utamaro made woodblock prints. This meant their paintings could be mass-produced, so that nearly everyone could afford them. The first prints were dull compared to the original paintings, but they became more colourful as printing methods improved.

At the end of the 19th century, ukiyo-e prints were often used to wrap Japanese ornaments and furniture on sale in Europe. Western artists had never seen ukiyo-e art before – and they loved it! The colours and compositions influenced artists such as Claude Monet, Edgar Degas and J. A. M. Whistler. Some ukiyo-e artists, such as Utagawa Hiroshige and Katsushika Hokusai, quickly became famous in the West.

3-second sum-up
Ukiyo-e were mass-produced pictures showing life in Japan.

3-minute mission **Make a string print**

You need: • Piece of card • Glue • String • Paper • Paints and paintbrushes • Rolling pin

Take a piece of card and glue a length of string to it in any shape or pattern you like – maybe a wave or a parasol. When the glue has dried, paint the string with fairly thick paint. Press a sheet of paper over it, hold it firmly and rub the soft edge of your hand over it or use a rolling pin. Then peel back the paper to reveal your picture.

Ukiyo-e woodblock prints showed scenes of everyday life in Japan.

An artist draws the outline of the design using ink.

A carver pastes the drawing on a block of wood and carves the design. This block is used to print the black outline of the picture.

More blocks are carved – one for each colour. These are called colour plates.

The printer paints the raised areas of each colour plate – one colour per block.

The printer then presses the paper on the painted colour plates and rolls over the back to print the design.

The process is repeated for each colour plate. Light colours are always printed first.

Although the process takes a lot of work, once the blocks are completed, it is easy to print the same design many times.

The Great Wave off Kanagawa, by Katsushika Hokusai, 1826–33

Impressionism
... in 30 seconds

In the 1860s, a group of young French artists, including Claude Monet, Camille Pissarro, Pierre-Auguste Renoir and Berthe Morisot, invented their own original artistic style. Rather than traditional, carefully composed paintings, they painted passing moments, using quick brushmarks to capture the effects of light.

Berthe Morisot
1841–95

Like the Realists and Landscape painters, the Impressionists painted (and some sculpted) people, landscapes and events in everyday life. Many painted in the open air. They were more interested in how light changes the colours of scenes at different times of day and in different weather conditions than in capturing details. They worked quickly, using short brushstrokes and bright colours. Several of them never used black.

At first, most people did not like Impressionism. It looked messy, as if the artists lacked skill. In 1874, the Impressionists organized their own exhibition. Many viewers simply laughed, while others were horrified. One critic commented that their work looked unfinished, and was just 'impressions'. That's how the Impressionists got their name. However, by the late 1880s, Impressionism had become popular and the artists became famous.

3-second sum-up

The Impressionists painted quickly, capturing fleeting moments, light and colour.

3-minute mission Make an impression

You need: • Paper • Paints and paintbrushes • Scissors • Glue • Green-coloured paper • White-coloured paper or tissue paper

Monet is famous for his water-lily paintings (look them up on the Internet if you can). Make your own by painting light and dark blue wavy lines across a sheet of paper. Leave some white paper showing through as sunlight sparkling on the water. When this is dry, glue on green paper 'lily pads'. Scrunch some white paper or tissue paper and glue these 'lilies' on to your green pads. Around these, paint darker green and blue reflections.

The Impressionists invented a style of art that was quick, bright and sometimes messy.

Artists often painted outdoors and worked quickly so they could capture brief moments in time and the effects of light and weather.

Some used rough brushstrokes and unmixed colours straight from the paint tubes.

They painted everyday subjects, often from unusual viewpoints.

Regattas at Argenteuil, by Claude Monet, c. 1872

Post-Impressionism
... in 30 seconds

After the Impressionists came the Post-Impressionists, who worked from around 1885 to 1910. Like the Impressionists, they were mainly French and they were interested in light, shadows and bold colours.

Unlike the Impressionists, they worked alone, trying out new ways of representing the world. This meant that the different artists developed unique styles and techniques. For example, Georges Seurat developed his own way of painting, building up his works with tiny dots rather than normal brushstrokes. This method is called Pointillism.

The Post-Impressionists often used bright colours, and artists including Vincent van Gogh and Georges Seurat placed complementary colours (colours that are opposite one another on the colour wheel) next to each other to make everything look brighter. Paul Gauguin painted flat, bright colours with dark outlines, and he sometimes used symbols to suggest double meanings. Henri de Toulouse-Lautrec painted people in Paris nightclubs using vivid colours and a fluid, flowing style. The painters' range of ideas had a huge impact on the artists who followed them, many of whom used colours and paint marks more expressively and less realistically.

3-second sum-up

Post-Impressionists had their own unique style and techniques, but colour was important to them all.

3-minute mission Paint like Van Gogh

You need: • Paper • Pencil • Paints and paintbrushes

On a sheet of paper, lightly draw the basic outlines of the trees, village and hills of Van Gogh's *The Starry Night*. Now, using only a little water, mix thick paint, and paint your own starry night using bold colours and obvious brushmarks. Leave areas of the paper white for stars and avoid mixing colours together if you can.

Post-Impressionists used bold colours and developed unique, distinctive painting techniques.

The colour wheel shows how colours are related to each other.

Blue, red and yellow are primary colours.

Green, purple and orange are secondary colours (made by mixing two primary colours together).

Blue and orange, which are complementary colours (opposite each other on the colour wheel), are placed next to each other to make everything look brighter.

Different artists used different techniques. Here, Van Gogh has laid the paint on so thickly that you can see the texture of the brushstrokes.

The Starry Night, by Vincent van Gogh, 1889

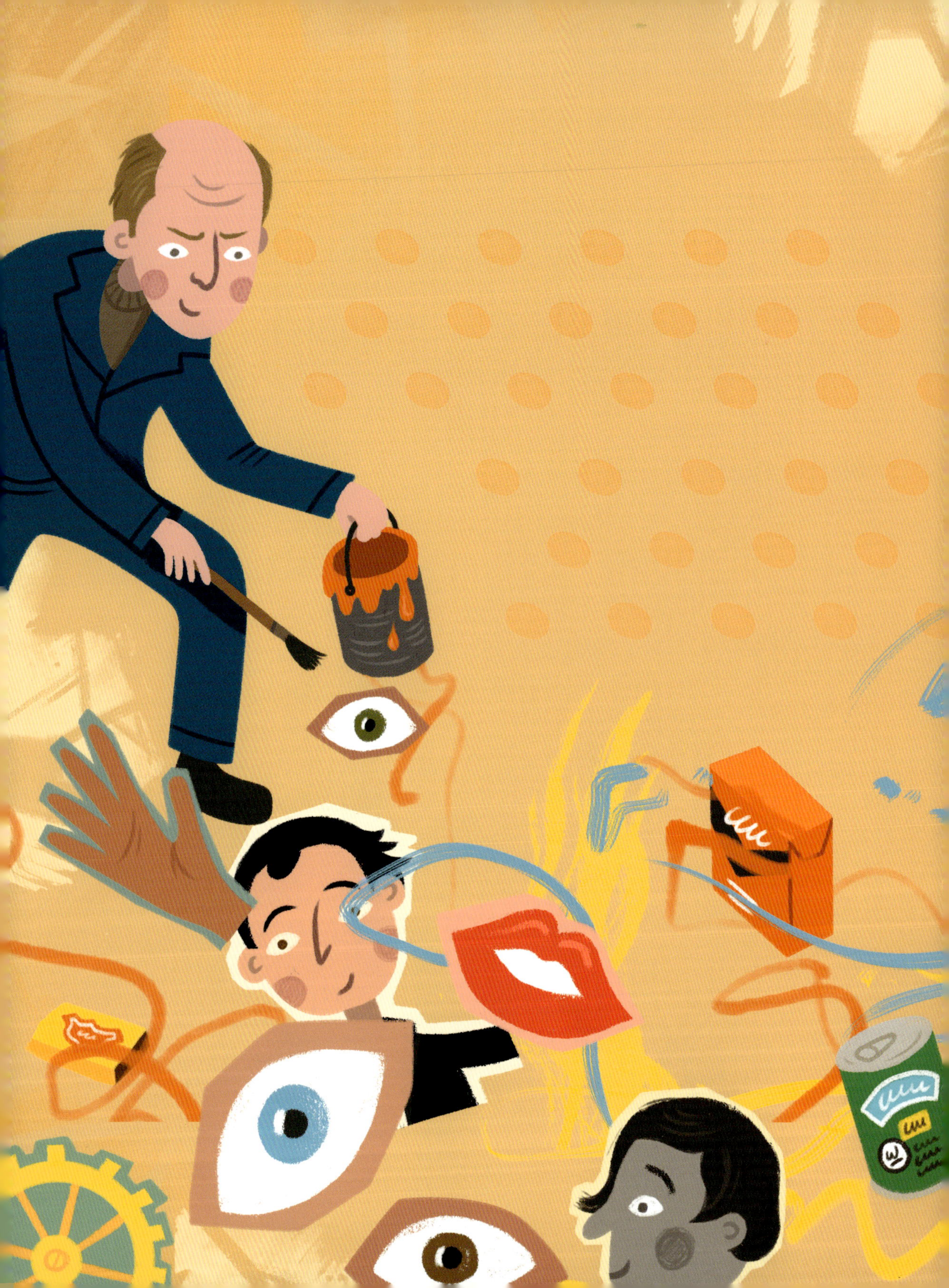

Modern art

Before the 20th century, there were lots of accepted rules about what artists could or should paint or sculpt, and the materials they could use. Then everything changed. The Impressionists had started it by challenging the rules. Photography had a lot to do with it too – if a camera could make an instant picture of the real world, why should an artist do the same? Soon, many artists began expressing themselves almost however they liked. Some decided not to make art that looked realistic and, for some, technical skills became less important. This sense of freedom allowed new ideas and art movements to form.

Modern art Glossary

abstract Not realistic or lifelike.

art movement A group of artists producing a similar style or type of art at a certain time.

automatism A way of creating art without thinking about it, using the **unconscious mind**.

canvas Cloth that is tightly stretched over wooden bars. Canvases are used as a surface for painting.

collage A technique in which paper, newspaper, cloth or other materials are cut up, arranged and stuck down to create an artwork.

exhibition A display of works of art, generally held in a gallery or museum.

flat colour Blocks of colour with little shading or shadow, which look 'flat' and **two-dimensional**.

geometric shape A regular, precise shape made out of straight or curving lines, such as a circle, rectangle or square. The opposite of a geometric shape is an organic shape, which is natural and irregular, with flowing lines.

manifesto A written statement that describes the aims and opinions of a person or group.

mass-produced Made in large amounts, often by machinery.

pastel A soft stick of colour that can be easily smudged or blended and is used for drawing.

perspective A way of drawing that shows depth and distance; this gives the impression that something drawn on a **two-dimensional** surface is **three-dimensional**.

Post-Impressionist The **art movement** that came after the Impressionists, from around 1885 to 1910. Post-Impressionist artists used a variety of styles, but were all interested in colour.

print An image made by pressing a carved block or plate, covered in ink or paint, on to paper. This technique allows lots of copies to be made of the same image.

Renaissance The revival of learning, art and literature in Europe during the 15th and 16th centuries, inspired by a new interest in ancient Greek and Roman cultures.

sculpture A **three-dimensional** piece of art, such as a statue, made from stone, wood, clay or another material.

subject What the artist has chosen to paint, draw or sculpt.

symbolism The use of symbols to show ideas. A symbol is something that represents another thing, for example, a skull in a painting might be a symbol for death.

three-dimensional (3D) Something that is not flat; it has height, depth and width.

two-dimensional (2D) Something that is flat; it has height and width, but not depth.

unconscious mind The part of the mind we are not aware of, but which still affects our feelings and behaviour.

Expressionism
... in 30 seconds

In the early 20th century, German artists began to create paintings and sculptures that showed their emotions. They were influenced by late 19th-century painters such as Edvard Munch and Vincent van Gogh. The artists used unusual colours and subjects that shocked many people. This new style of art became known as Expressionism.

The Expressionist movement began mainly in Germany, but later spread throughout Europe. In 1905 in Dresden, Germany, a group of Expressionists described their art as a bridge between the past and the future, calling themselves Die Brücke (The Bridge). The artists in the group included Ernst Ludwig Kirchner, Emil Nolde and Karl Schmidt-Rottluff. They used bold, unnatural colours – such as blue or yellow for a person's skin – and contorted shapes to express their feelings. They felt disturbed by the greed and selfishness they saw, and their art aimed to pass on these same disturbed feelings to viewers.

In 1911, the artists Wassily Kandinsky and Franz Marc formed another Expressionist group, called Der Blaue Reiter (The Blue Rider). Kandinsky said that the name came from their shared love of horses and from the colour blue, which he thought was a spiritual colour. Der Blaue Reiter artists also used bold colours and strange shapes to express their thoughts and feelings.

3-second sum-up

By distorting shapes and colours, Expressionists showed their feelings, not reality.

3-minute mission Be an Expressionist

You need: • White, coloured or black paper • Pastels • Friend or family member

Ask a friend or family member to pull a face and really 'feel' that emotion. It could be fear, anger, sorrow, confusion or happiness for instance. On a sheet of paper, use pastels to draw what you see, exaggerating the features and colours to emphasize the emotion. Don't spend ages on it – your first impressions are often the most powerful.

Instead of trying to create accurate copies of what they saw, the Expressionists painted how they felt.

Ernst Ludwig Kirchner used bold, unexpected colours for people's faces, hair and clothes, and distorted shapes for their bodies.

Expressionist art was often purposely strange and disturbing to look at.

Street Scene, by Ernst Ludwig Kirchner, 1913

Cubism
... in 30 seconds

Cubism was influenced by African art and also by the earlier Post-Impressionist artist Paul Cézanne, who explored the underlying structures of things in his paintings. The style was first called Cubism by a journalist who remarked that the paintings looked like they were made of 'little cubes'.

Pablo Picasso
1881-1973

The first Cubists were the Spanish artist Pablo Picasso and the French artist Georges Braque. Painters had been following the rules of perspective since the Renaissance to create flat paintings that looked three-dimensional (3D), but the Cubists wanted to find a new way of showing their subjects. Instead of using perspective, they painted things from several angles at once. This made most Cubist paintings look as if they were made up of broken fragments and angles, as different sides and parts of the subject are shown in one image.

Because Cubist paintings are full of shapes and angles, most artists used only a few colours – such as browns, blues and greys – to make the pictures less confusing. Often, only the most important parts of a subject were painted to help viewers see it more clearly. From 1912, Picasso and Braque also began using collage. They glued materials, such as cloth or newspaper, on to their paintings to show different parts of a subject. This became called Synthetic Cubism.

3-second sum-up

Cubists abandoned the rules of perspective to try to show the 3D world on a flat canvas.

3-minute mission Make a Cubist collage

You need: • Magazines or printouts from the Internet • Scissors • Paper or card • Glue • Pencil or pen

Find two or three pictures – in magazines or from the Internet – of the same subject. Cut them up and rearrange them on a sheet of paper or card. When you are happy with your arrangement, glue them down. If you like, add some lines or marks to show other parts of your subject.

Cubists painted one subject from different angles to show 3D objects in 2D paintings.

This painting of a violin shows the instrument from various angles.

Abandoning techniques of perspective, Cubists painted the structure of things rather than a rigid image from one viewpoint.

Only a few colours are used to stop the painting becoming too difficult to understand.

Violin and Palette, by Georges Braque, c. 1909–10

Futurism
... in 30 seconds

In the early 20th century, some Italian artists became excited about the latest inventions, such as cars and planes. They wanted to create new paintings, sculpture, poetry and architecture that celebrated machines, speed, energy, power and the future. They called their movement Futurism.

Futurists weren't interested in the art of the past. In 1909, the Italian writer Filippo Tommaso Marinetti wrote a manifesto (a statement) about Futurism. He explained the Futurists' opinions, and declared that everything in Italian galleries, museums and libraries should be destroyed to make way for this new art form. This didn't happen in the end, but it showed that the Futurists wanted their art to ignore the past and focus on the future.

Futurists liked to show movement and use bright colours. The painter and sculptor Umberto Boccioni thought that all moving things had 'force lines' – lines of energy running through them as they travelled. He showed these lines in his sculptures and paintings.

3-second sum-up

Using colour, line and shape, Futurists celebrated technology, machines, speed and movement.

3-minute mission Painting movement

You need: • Coloured paper • Pencil • Pastels • Paintbrush or tissue

On coloured paper, use a pencil to lightly draw an animal or a person walking or running. Now, with pastels, apply broken strokes or diagonal lines (not blocks) in vivid colours, then use your hand or a dry paintbrush or tissue to smudge the pastels away from the moving animal or person.

Futurists focused on looking forward and celebrated everything that was new, fast and powerful.

Several Futurists captured the energy of movement by painting 'force lines'.

Here, a man rushes past on a horse. The force lines show that the horse and the rider are moving forwards, as well as up and down. There are smoky industrial factories in the background, celebrating machinery and industrial progress.

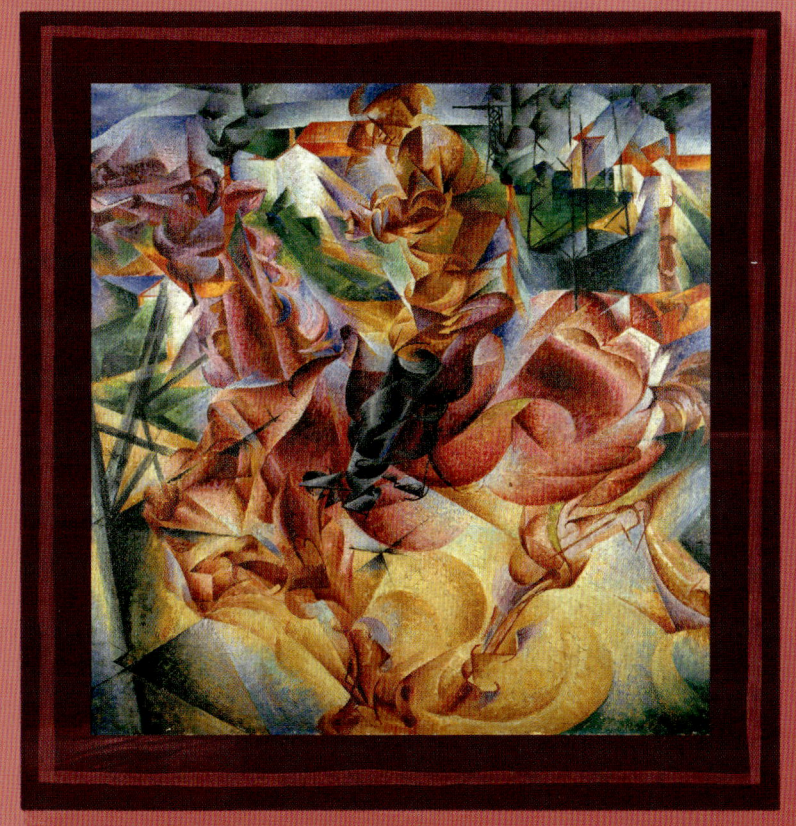

Elasticity, by Umberto Boccioni, 1912

Dada
... in 30 seconds

When World War I broke out in 1914, several European artists moved to Zurich, in Switzerland, because it was a neutral country – it did not take a side in the fighting.

Hearing about the war from the safety of Switzerland, the artists were appalled that people were killing each other so brutally and heartlessly. They began protesting about it by producing 'anti-art': images, sculptures, music, writing and performances that deliberately did not make sense, because the war made no sense to them.

**Hannah Höch
1889-1978**

The artists called their movement Dada. It was a random name, chosen because it meant nothing to anyone. The ideas soon spread to France, Germany, Spain and the USA, and the movement continued until about 1920.

The Dadaists made fun of artistic traditions and liked to shock viewers. They often used materials not normally used in art – German artists Hannah Höch and Max Ernst made collages out of rubbish they found. Some Dadaists presented ordinary objects as art in exhibitions and, at one exhibition, a pianist put on a performance where he didn't play a single note!

3-second sum-up

Dada was 'nonsense art', deliberately ridiculous, to protest against the horrors of war.

Readymades

In 1917, Marcel Duchamp tried to exhibit a urinal in an art exhibition. He turned it upside down, signed it 'R. Mutt', and called it *Fountain*. He believed that the fact that he had not made the urinal did not mean that it was not art. By showing it in an art gallery, he knew that people would look at it in a different way. Although it angered many people at the time, it had a huge impact on art that followed. Duchamp had started the idea that 'readymades', or things that had already been made for other purposes, could be used in art.

The Dadaists created purposely senseless art that reflected the senseless killings in World War I.

Rejecting the materials and methods of traditional art, the Dadaists aimed to shock viewers and challenge their ideas about what could be called art.

Artist Marcel Duchamp used existing objects to make his unusual art pieces. These were called 'readymades'.

Collage was an important technique for Dada artists. The collages didn't try to tell a clear story and they showed that things found in everyday life could be turned into art.

Bicycle Wheel, by Marcel Duchamp, 1951 (after lost original of 1913)

Surrealism
... in 30 seconds

In 1924, a new movement of writers and artists began in Paris. It was called Surrealism and was led by a poet called André Breton. Surrealism means 'more than real', or 'above real', and the Surrealists were interested in creating art and literature that showed the unconscious mind – the part of the mind that we are not aware of.

Breton had been inspired by the Austrian psychoanalyst Sigmund Freud. Freud was one of the first people to explore the unconscious mind. He studied memories, dreams and instincts and decided that many important thoughts and true feelings lie hidden in our unconscious minds.

Surrealists created weird-looking art, with odd things placed together. They made art in two main ways. One was carefully planned and showed everyday things in realistic ways, but in dream-like situations. The other way, called automatism, meant the artist created a work 'automatically' – without thinking about it, as if it had sprung from his or her unconscious mind.

René Magritte 1898–1967

Salvador Dalí, René Magritte and Yves Tanguy worked in the first way, while Joan Miró, Paul Klee and Jean Arp often worked using automatism.

3-second sum-up
Surrealism expressed hidden thoughts of the unconscious mind.

3-minute mission Automatism

You need: • Large sheet of plain paper • Thick colouring pens • Paints and paintbrushes or colouring pencils

With a large sheet of plain paper in front of you, clear your mind. Try not to think about anything (it's not as easy as you might think). Take some thick colouring pens and doodle all over the paper, still not thinking about anything. After a while, stop, look at what you have done and colour in some of your doodle, either using more colouring pens or using paints or colouring pencils.

Surrealists often painted pictures that looked illogical, but fascinating. They were often based on their own dreams, nightmares, memories and even instincts.

Surrealist art often shows everyday objects in strange situations or places. In this painting by Salvador Dalí, there are giant melting clocks on a beach.

Artists were interested in dreams and the unconscious mind – a part of the mind that people aren't normally aware of.

The Persistence of Memory, by Salvador Dalí, 1931

Abstract Expressionism
... in 30 seconds

After World War II, in the 1940s and 1950s, a new art movement called Abstract Expressionism emerged in America. Abstract Expressionists wanted to create art that not only showed viewers how they felt about world problems, but also expressed their innermost thoughts.

Like the Surrealists, the Abstract Expressionists aimed to make art that came from the unconscious mind. The paintings didn't show objects or people, but used colours, brushstrokes and shapes to express the artists' feelings. The reaction of the people viewing the art was also important.

Abstract Expressionist artwork was usually huge, and paintings came in two main styles. Action painters, such as Jackson Pollock, Lee Krasner and Willem de Kooning, often used automatism to create their work, like some Surrealists had done. Other artists, such as Mark Rothko, Clyfford Still and Barnett Newman, used a more controlled painting style that was later called Colour Field painting. There was also Abstract Expressionist sculpture.

Lee Krasner 1908-84

Action painter Jackson Pollock would lay a canvas on the floor and, without any planning, he would splash, throw and dribble paint on to it straight from large cans. Colour Field artists soaked canvases with large areas – or fields – of colour.

3-second sum-up

Abstract Expressionism featured huge, abstract works that expressed the artists' emotions.

3-minute mission Be an Abstract Expressionist!

You need: • Large sheet of thick paper • Paints • Drinking straw, or cocktail stick or cotton bud

Put a blob of paint on thick paper. Concentrate on how you feel and either blow on it through a straw or 'draw' lines and shapes with it using a cocktail stick or cotton bud. Turn the paper round and work from different angles. Add another blob of colour nearby and do the same again, and then again with a third colour.

Abstract Expressionists didn't try to copy the real world, but instead showed their feelings using colour and shape.

Because Abstract Expressionist artworks are abstract, they can mean completely different things to different people.

Colour Field paintings, like this one by Rothko, normally have large, flat areas of plain colours, and they're often huge.

Jackson Pollock didn't plan his paintings. He let his unconscious mind take over and painted spontaneously.

Untitled, by Mark Rothko, 1952

Pop art
... in 30 seconds

Pop art was a fun art movement that began in the 1950s in London and spread to New York in the 1960s. Pop artists were fed up with the snobbery that surrounded art, particularly Abstract Expressionism. They wanted to make art that everyone could enjoy. Their works were based on everyday, familiar things, such as packaging, labels, comics, advertising and celebrities.

Some Pop artists created pictures using materials and methods that had never before been used for art. The British artist Richard Hamilton cut up images from magazines to create collages set in people's homes. In America, the artist Andy Warhol used bright, flat colours and copied the printing methods of advertising and comic books. His repeating images reminded viewers of the mass-produced goods in supermarkets.

Although all Pop art focused on the modern world, every artist's work was different. Andy Warhol made huge pictures of cans of soup and film stars. Claes Oldenburg made large, squishy sculptures of burgers and ice cream. Roy Lichtenstein made paintings that looked like huge comic strips. Everyone could enjoy these bright images, whether or not they knew about art.

3-second sum-up

Pop art was inspired by adverts, packaging and comics and was meant to be an extension of the modern life that everyone experienced.

3-minute mission Pop art pictures

You need: • A5 and A3 paper • Pencil • Scanner and printer • Glue • Colouring pencils, pens or paints and paintbrushes

Design some food packaging – perhaps a bar of chocolate, a tin of baked beans or a cereal packet. Using just pencil outlines, make the design clear and simple and then scan it and print it four times on to A5-sized paper. Glue the four identical designs on to a piece of A3 paper, one filling each quarter. Using colouring pencils, pens or paints, colour in all four pictures differently, using bright, unnatural colours.

Pop art reflected real life in the 1950s and 1960s and was meant for everyone to enjoy.

Bright, flat colours were used.

Images and patterns were often repeated.

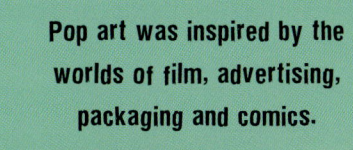

Pop art was inspired by the worlds of film, advertising, packaging and comics.

Campbell's Soup Cans, by Andy Warhol, 1965

Minimalism
... in 30 seconds

Although the term 'Minimalism' had been used already, it became particularly popular during the 1960s to 1970s to describe a new style of art that started in New York and then spread and continued into the 21st century. Focusing on precision, balance and calmness, Minimalism was almost opposite to the random and colourful approach of Abstract Expressionism.

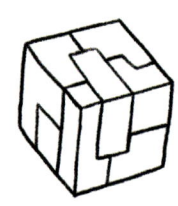

Instead of using paint, Minimalists often used modern industrial materials such as wooden blocks, house bricks, metals or fluorescent lights. Minimalist artists created simple, three-dimensional (3D) artworks using geometric shapes. They often made patterns by repeating their 3D shapes, while always keeping their art to a minimum of only the essential elements. They wanted their art to be just about materials and shapes, nothing else.

Minimalist art was often large, and the combination of its simplicity and its huge size meant that viewers noticed the space around it as well as the work itself. This space was part of the art. Famous Minimalists include Donald Judd, who used machine-made materials to create art that was meant to be free of emotion, and Carl Andre, who places objects, such as bricks, in regular arrangements to make us think about shapes and materials.

3-second sum-up

Minimalism was about everyday, often industrial, materials used as art in simple shapes and structures.

3-minute mission
Make a minimalist artwork

You need: • Toy bricks or cardboard boxes

Design your own Minimalist artwork using toy bricks or cardboard boxes. Work out an arrangement using repeated patterns and simple shapes. Remember, you can leave spaces in between the shapes if you like.

For Minimalists, less was more.

Artists often used modern, industrial materials, such as...

Metal

Wood

Bricks

Fluorescent lights

Minimalism was often just about the shapes, the materials and the space around the art. It didn't have a message or a story to tell.

Using 3D shapes and repeated patterns, Minimalist art aimed to be as simple as possible.

Untitled, by Donald Judd, 1989

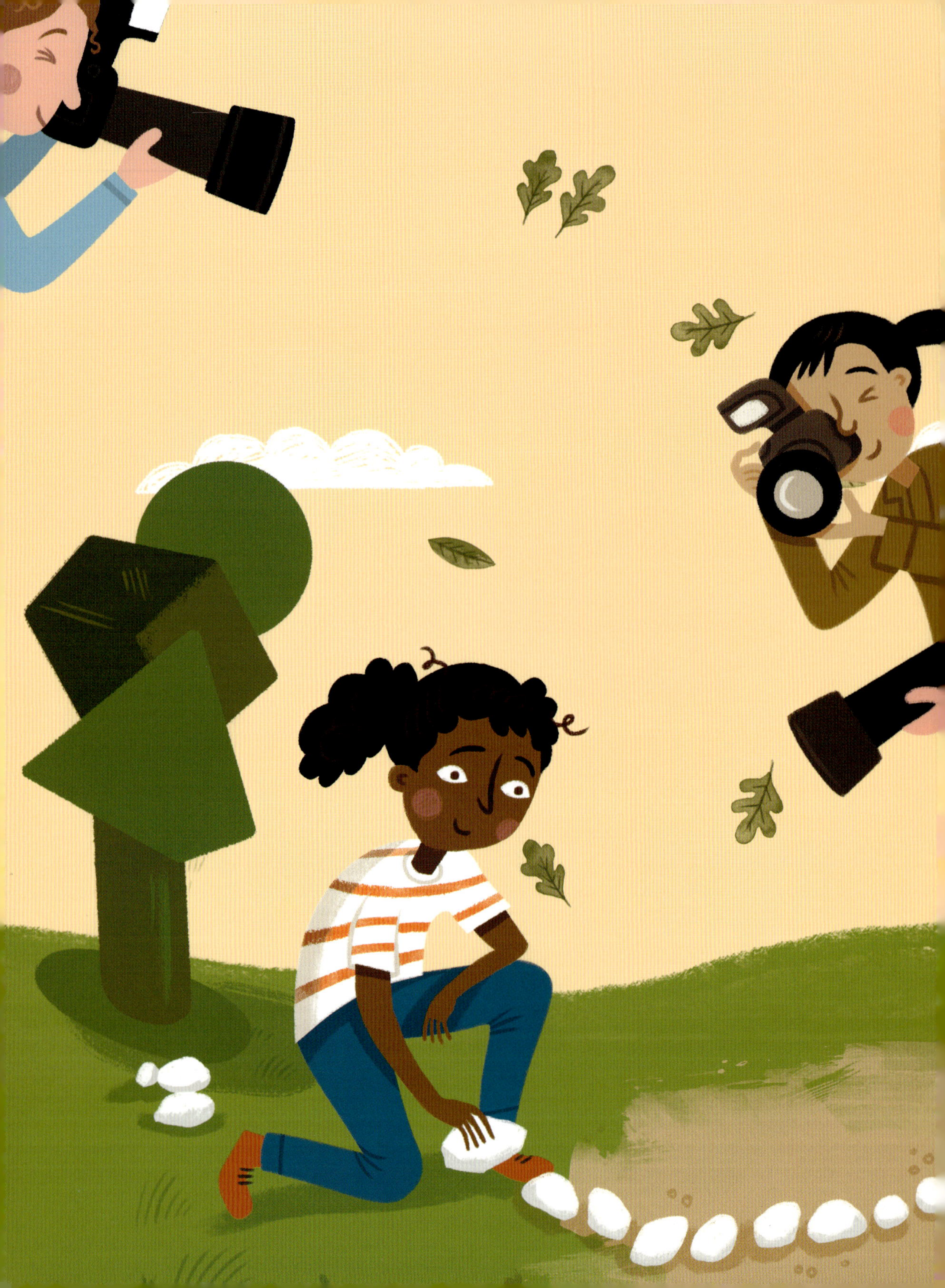

Contemporary art

By the 1970s, artists began using a broader range of materials. Unexpected objects such as household items, computers or building materials found their way into works of art. Some artists even used the natural world around them. Art became less about technique and more about ideas – and that's still true today. Works of art can be shocking, puzzling or funny. In contemporary art, viewers' reactions are often as important as the art itself.

Contemporary art
Glossary

environmentalist A person who is concerned with protecting the environment.

installation A large, three-dimensional construction made from different **media**, that is often temporary and designed for a certain space; an installation might take up a whole room of a gallery.

land art Art that is created directly in the landscape, using natural materials.

mass-produced Made in large amounts, often by machinery.

media The material used by an artist to make an artwork, such as oil paints, pastels or clay.

performance art Artworks that are created by the actions of the artist, audience or other performers, in a live or recorded performance.

prehistoric From prehistory (the period of time before writing was invented).

sculpture A three-dimensional piece of art, such as a statue, made from stone, wood, clay or another material.

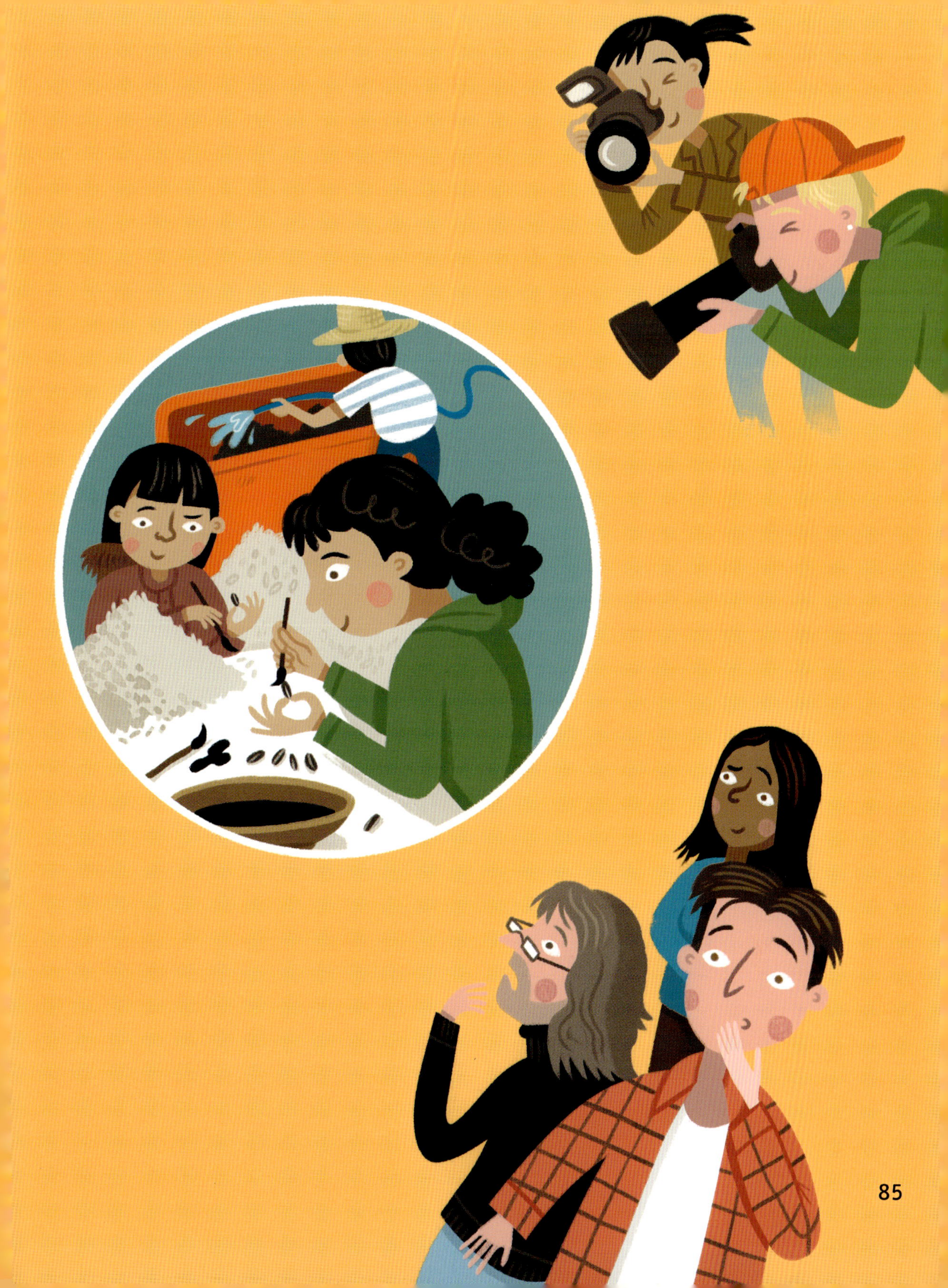

Land art

... in 30 seconds

For thousands of years, artists have painted pictures and made sculptures that show the world around us. But Land artists use the natural world itself to create their artworks. This new way of making art began in the USA in the late 1960s.

Land artists were inspired by natural objects, and also by the cave art created by prehistoric artists. Some Land artists didn't agree with the high prices and snobbery of the art world. They liked the idea of using simple, natural materials, and making art that could not be bought or exhibited.

Most Land artists work outdoors using materials they find, such as rocks, leaves and gravel. Their art is often temporary. Some simply walk through a landscape or move objects, such as stones or leaves, slightly. They take photos or make maps, and then often leave the land as it was before they arrived. Most Land artists care about the environment – they would never damage it.

The American artist, Robert Smithson, built a huge spiral jetty out of earth and stones in the Great Salt Lake in Utah, USA. British artist Richard Long is famous for taking long walks in open spaces, photographing and making maps of his journey. British artist Andy Goldsworthy is a sculptor and environmentalist who creates artworks out of stone, sticks, mud and leaves.

3-second sum-up

Land art, which is often deliberately temporary, uses natural materials to make people think about the environment.

3-minute mission Land art gallery

Collect a few small things from outside, such as leaves, pebbles, shells, acorns, twigs, daisies or fir cones. Only use things you find lying around and don't take anything from places where they should stay. Check with an adult if you're not sure. Find a small space and make a design using your objects, perhaps on grass or sand. Try a circle, spiral or wiggly line. Take a photo of it if you can.

Instead of copying the world around us, Land artists use it to create art.

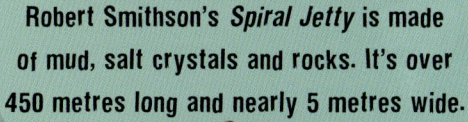

Robert Smithson's *Spiral Jetty* is made of mud, salt crystals and rocks. It's over 450 metres long and nearly 5 metres wide.

This sculpture by Andy Goldsworthy is entirely made from natural stone, carefully piled up into the shape of an egg.

Rocks, leaves, sticks, stones, or even ice, snow and water, can all be used to make Land art.

Left: *Spiral Jetty*, by Robert Smithson, 1970
Right: *Sentinel*, by Andy Goldsworthy, 1998

Conceptualism

... in 30 seconds

Art nowadays frequently focuses on being original, and surprising viewers with unexpected ideas or ways of showing them. Starting in the 1960s, several artists decided that the concepts – ideas – behind art were more important than what art looks like. This was the start of the Conceptual art movement.

Conceptualism developed because the artists were angry that art was becoming just another expensive thing that only rich people could afford. They also decided that traditional artistic skills were seen as more important than they should be. By making ideas more important than either price or skill, they thought they were freeing art, as no one can buy or sell an idea.

Conceptualists use whatever techniques and materials they feel show their ideas best. The German artist Joseph Beuys used lots of felt. He said that tribesmen had wrapped him in felt and fat during World War II to stop him freezing to death after his fighter plane had crashed. This idea became an important element of some of his art. In 2005, American Conceptualist Mary Kelly asked young women to help her re-create historical photographs of demonstrations from the 1970s. Her ideas came from her beliefs about women's rights.

3-second sum-up

Conceptualist art focuses on the ideas behind art, rather than technical skill.

Art of the mind

Conceptual artists, or Conceptualists, are not like artists of the past who focused on their technical skills. Many Conceptualists use or show different sorts of skills that have not always been recognised in art, or they create massive artworks so viewers have to take part in the idea. Some of the ideas come from artists' personal experiences and some come from the world around them, but it's always about seeing and thinking about things from another point of view.

Conceptualists believe that the ideas behind art are more important than what the art looks like.

Artist Ai Weiwei created an installation made of 100 million hand-painted porcelain sunflower seeds.

His idea was to make people think about mass production, individual skills and traditional Chinese crafts.

Japanese artist Yayoi Kusama is best known for her huge installations and sculptures covered in dots.

The idea comes from Kusama's personal life. She sometimes has hallucinations and she tries to make sense of this by turning her visions into real objects covered in dots.

Top: *Sunflower Seeds*, by Ai Weiwei, 2011
Bottom: *Pumpkin*, by Yayoi Kusama, 2006

New media art
... in 30 seconds

At the end of the 20th century and into the 21st century, many artists turned away from traditional painting and sculpture to experiment with new materials (also sometimes called media) such as video, digital art, computer graphics, computer animation, virtual art, Internet art and 3D printing.

Art made of unusual materials often challenges what we expect and gives artists opportunities to create an even wider variety of art. For example, digital art can be computer-generated, scanned or drawn on a tablet or mobile phone.

Some contemporary artists purposely make art that provokes strong reactions among viewers. In the 1990s, British artist Damien Hirst displayed dead animals in glass tanks filled with formaldehyde, a liquid chemical that stops things from rotting. The strong opinions and reactions viewers had about Hirst's work became a major feature of the art, and so even more people heard about it, and Hirst became well known.

Some artists like to inspire controversy – strong reactions and opinions – from viewers. This isn't because they want to cause arguments, but because they want people to question the ideas behind art, and not just to rely on what experts say.

3-second sum-up

Art now is made of all kinds of materials that are often used to make viewers think in new ways.

Clocks

In 1991, Cuban-born artist Felix Gonzalez-Torres exhibited two identical battery-operated clocks. He started them at exactly the same time, but because nothing is ever exactly the same, eventually the batteries – and clocks – fell out of time with each other. Gonzalez-Torres wanted viewers to think about the strong bonds between people who love each other, and about how eventually, over time, all our lives go in different directions.

Artists today use a huge range of materials and some create controversial artworks.

Damien Hirst's art installations use non-traditional art materials, including dead animals and chemicals.

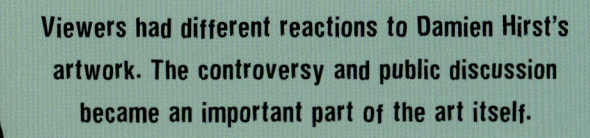

Viewers had different reactions to Damien Hirst's artwork. The controversy and public discussion became an important part of the art itself.

The Physical Impossibility of Death in the Mind of Someone Living, by Damien Hirst, 1991

Discover more

NON-FICTION BOOKS

13 Art Movements Children Should Know by Brad Finger, Prestel, 2014

13 Artists Children Should Know by Angela Wenzel, Prestel, 2009

Book of Famous Artists, Usborne, 2014

Children's Book of Art by Rosie Dickins, Usborne, 2005

My Big Art Show by Susie Hodge, Thames & Hudson, 2014

The Art Book for Children, Phaidon, 2005

The Art Book for Children, Book 2 by Amanda Renshaw, Phaidon, 2007

The Children's Interactive Story of Art by Susie Hodge, Carlton Kids, 2015

The Short Story of Art by Susie Hodge, Laurence King, 2017

Van Gogh and the Post-Impressionists for Kids by Carol Sabbeth, Zephyr Press, 2011

Vincent's Starry Night and Other Stories: A Children's History of Art by Michael Bird and Kate Evans, Laurence King, 2016

Why is Art Full of Naked People? by Susie Hodge, Thames & Hudson, 2016

FICTION BOOKS

Katie and the Impressionists by James Mayhew, Orchard Books, 2014

Klimt and his Cat by Berenice Capatti, Wm. B. Eerdmans Publishing, 2004

Leonardo and the Flying Boy by Laurence Anholt, Frances Lincoln Children's Books, 2016

Modern Art Mayhem by Susie Hodge, QEB, 2017

Picasso's Trousers by Nicholas Allen, Red Fox Picture Books, 2012

The Magical Tree by Myrian Ouyessad and Anja Klauss, Prestel, 2016

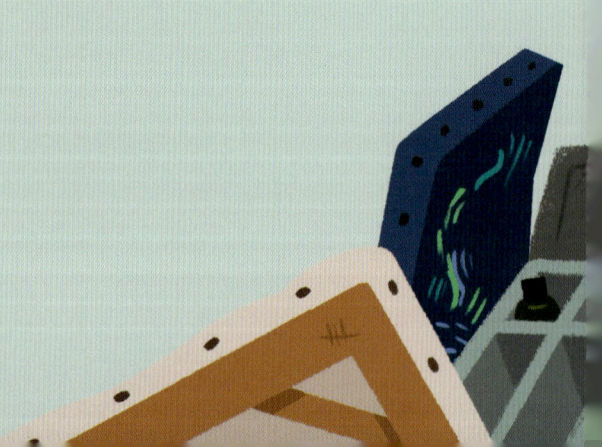

APPS

Art Authority by Open Door Networks, Inc.

Art Museum (Match'Em Up™ History & Geography) by EnsenaSoft

iMuseum Musée d'Orsay by Utagoe Inc.

Love Art: National Gallery, London by Antenna Audio Inc.

NGAKids Art Zone by National Gallery of Art, Washington

Uffizi by Parallelo

WEBSITES

Google Art Project, www.google.com/culturalinstitute/project/art-project

MetKids, www.metmuseum.org/collection/metkids/

http://www.colormatters.com/

http://www.ducksters.com/history/art/

http://kids.tate.org.uk/

http://www.nga.gov/content/ngaweb/education/kids.html

Although every endeavour has been made by the publisher to ensure that all content from these websites is educational material of the highest quality and is age appropriate, we strongly advise that Internet access is supervised by a responsible adult.

Index

abstract art **76–7**
Action Painting **76–7**
animals **22–3, 25, 32–3, 43, 71, 90–1**
architecture **27, 28, 32, 44, 46–7**
Arp, Jean **74**
automatism **64, 74, 76**

Beuys, Joseph **88**
Bible, the **30–1, 44–5**
Blaue Reiter, Der **66**
Boccioni, Umberto **70–1**
Botticelli **38**
Boucher, François **46**
Braque, Georges **68–9**
Breton, André **74**
Brücke, Die **66**
Bruegel, Pieter (the Elder) **40–1**

Caravaggio **44–5**
cave art **22–3, 86**
Cézanne, Paul **68**
chiaroscuro **44**
collage **64, 68, 72–3, 78**
Colour Field painting **76–7**
colour wheel **60–1**
complementary colours **60–1**
Constable, John **54**
Courbet, Gustave **54**

Dalí, Salvador **74–5**
David, Jacques-Louis **52–3**
Degas, Edgar **56**
Delacroix, Eugène **52–3**
Donatello **38**
Duchamp, Marcel **72–3**
Dürer, Albrecht **40–1**

El Greco **42–3**
engravings **36, 40**
Ernst, Max **72**
exhibitions **58, 72**

film **90**
force lines **70**
frescoes **20–1, 28–9, 30**

Gauguin, Paul **60**
Géricault, Théodore **52**
Giorgio Martini, Francesco di **39**
Goldsworthy, Andy **86–7**
Gonzalez-Torres, Felix **90**
Goya, Francisco de **52**

Hamilton, Richard **78**
Hiroshige, Utagawa **56**
Hirst, Damien **90–1**
Höch, Hannah **72**
Hokusai, Katsushika **56–7**
Holbein, Hans (the Younger) **40**

icons 30
illuminated manuscripts 20, 30–1
Industrial Revolution 49, 50, 54–5
Ingres, Jean-Auguste-Dominique 52
installations 84, 88–9, 90–1
interior design 36, 46–7

Kandinsky, Wassily 66
Kelly, Mary 88
Kirchner, Ernst Ludwig 66–7
Klee, Paul 74
Klimt, Gustav 92
Kooning, Willem de 76
Kusama, Yayoi 89

land art 86–7
landscapes 36, 46, 54–5, 56, 58–9
Lichtenstein, Roy 78
Long, Richard 86

Magritte, René 74
Manet, Édouard 54
Marc, Franz 66
Michelangelo 38
Millet, Jean-François 54–5
Miró, Joan 74
Monet, Claude 56, 58–9
Morisot, Berthe 58

mosaics 20, 28–9, 30–1
Munch, Edvard 66
myths 38

natural world 40, 46, 53, 86–7
Newman, Barnett 76
Nolde, Emil 66

oil paints 36, 40, 49
Oldenburg, Claes 78

paints 36–7, 36–7, 40, 49, 50–1 52, 54
pastels 21, 22, 64, 66, 70, 84
performance art 72, 84, 90
performing arts 10, 13
perspective 36, 38–9, 68–9
photography 13, 63, 86, 90
Picasso, Pablo 68, 92
pictographs 32
pigments 37, 40
Pissarro, Camille 58
pointillism 60
Pollock, Jackson 76–7
portraits 37, 40, 42, 46, 53, 78
pottery 26–7, 28, 32
primary colours 61
prints 37, 40–1, 56–7, 78–9
proportion 21, 26–7, 42

Index

Raphael **38**
readymades **72–3**
reliefs **21, 28–9, 32**
religious art **30–1, 42**
Rembrandt, Harmenszoon van Rijn **44**
Renoir, Pierre-Auguste **58**
Rothko, Mark **76–7**

Schmidt-Rottluff, Karl **66**
sculpture **10, 12–13, 21, 26–7, 28–9, 32–3, 38, 44, 70, 72–3, 78, 84, 86–7**
secondary colours **61**
Seurat, Georges **60**
sfumato **38**
Smithson, Robert **86–7**
statues **22, 26–7, 28, 32**
Still, Clyfford **76**

Tanguy, Yves **74**
Titian **38**

Toulouse-Lautrec, Henri de **60**
Turk, Gavin **12**
Turner, J. M. W. **54**

unconscious mind **65, 74–5, 76–7**

Van Gogh, Vincent **17, 60–1, 66**
Vigée Le Brun, Elisabeth Louise **52**
Vinci, Leonardo da **16, 38, 92**

wall paintings **24–5, 28–9**
Warhol, Andy **78–9**
watercolours **54, 37**
Watteau, Jean-Antoine **46–7**
Weiwei, Ai **88–9**
Whistler, J. A. M. **56**
woodblocks **51, 56–7**
woodcuts **36, 40–1**
World War I **70, 72**
World War II **76, 88**

Picture Credits

p23 (top): Wikimedia Commons/Francesco Bandarin; p23 (bottom): Shutterstock/Eduardo Rivero; p25: Alamy/World History Archive; p27: Walters Art Museum; p29: Marie-Lan Nguyen; p31: Shutterstock/Vincent St. Thomas; p33: Walters Art Museum; p39 (left): Alamy/Heritage Image Partnership Ltd; p39 (right): Alamy/EmmePi Images; p41 (bottom) & p43: National Gallery of Art, Washington, D.C.; p45: The Metropolitan Museum of Art; p47: National Gallery of Art, Washington, D.C.; p53 (top): J. Paul Getty Museum. Digital image courtesy of the Getty's Open Content Program.; p53 (bottom): Shutterstock/Everett Art; p55: J. Paul Getty Museum. Digital image courtesy of the Getty's Open Content Program; p57: Library of Congress, Washington, D.C.; p59: Alamy/Granger Historical Picture Archive; p67: Bridgeman Images/Christie's Images; p69: Alamy/Granger Historical Picture Archive © ADAGP, Paris and DACS, London 2017; p71: Getty Images/Leemage/Corbis; p73: Scala, Florence/The Museum of Modern Art, New York © Succession Marcel; Duchamp/ADAGP, Paris and DACS, London 2017; p75: Alamy/Martin Shields © Salvador Dali, Fundació Gala-Salvador Dalí, DACS; p77: Bridgeman Images/Dallas Museum of Art, Texas, USA, gift of the Meadows Foundation, Incorporated © 1998 Kate Rothko Prizel & Christopher Rothko ARS, NY and DACS, London; p79: Bridgeman Images/Private Collection © 2017 The Andy Warhol Foundation for the Visual Arts, Inc./Artists Rights Society (ARS), New York and DACS, London; p81: Bridgeman Images/Private Collection © Judd Foundation/ARS, NY and DACS, London 2017; p87 (right): Getty Images/Camille Moirenc; p87 (left): Getty Images/George Steinmetz; p89 (top): Alamy/Reuters; p89 (bottom): Alamy/Chris Willson; p91: Artimage/Photo: Prudence Cuming Associates Ltd © Damien Hirst and Science Ltd. All rights reserved, DACS 2017.